Simple Soulwinning Steps

Practical Tips for Personal Evangelism

Published By

Help4U Publications
Chesterton, IN

Help4U
Publications

Simple Soulwinning Steps: Practical Tips for Personal Evangelism by David J. Olson

Copyright©2021 by David J. Olson

ISBN 978-1-940089-45-4

Library of Congress Control Number: 2021908068

www.help4Upublications.com

Credits: Photo from Canstockphoto.com

All rights reserved. No part of this publication may be reproduced or transmitted in any form, except for brief quotation in review, without written permission from the publisher.

All Scripture quotations are from the *King James Bible*.

DEDICATION

To my Dad, Roger Olson –

Since I can remember, you have had a burden for reaching the lost with the gospel, leading scores of people to the Lord and training many soulwinners. Truly, you have fruit that remains.

Your example has been a motivation to me over the years. I find myself putting into practice many of the lessons that I've learned from you. Therefore, your influence is mingled throughout the pages of this book. Thank you for your faithfulness.
With much love,
Dave

CONTENTS

Preface 7

Introduction: How to Use This Book 9

Part One: What to Do

    Lesson 1: Stop and Think 15

    Lesson 2: Get Ready 31

    Lesson 3: Follow God's Plan 47

    Lesson 4: Fill Your Heart and Head 65

    Lesson 5: Be Flexible 71

    Lesson 6: Anticipate Objections 81

Part Two: What to Say

    Lesson 7: God Loves Us, Not Our Sin 93

    Lesson 8: Sin Has to Be Punished 101

    Lesson 9: Good Works Don't Save 109

    Lesson 10: Repentance Is Required 117

    Lesson 11: Jesus Took Our Place 137

    Lesson 12: We Must Trust Jesus 145

    Lesson 13: Salvation Is Forever 157

    Lesson 14: There Is Much to Learn 167

Appendix A: Witnessing Helps 177

Appendix B: Ideas for Witnessing to the Non-Religious 179

PREFACE

Few things that we do in life will count more for eternity than winning souls to Christ. Jesus went out of His way to win souls. In fact, He said, *"I must be about my Father's business"* (Luke 2:49). Since we have been commanded to *"follow his steps"* (1 Peter 2:21), we must also be about our Father's business and evangelize lost souls around us.

Although most Christians know that they should tell the lost about Jesus, many fail to do it on a consistent basis. There are two basic reasons why believers don't witness: either they are unwilling, or they think that they are unable. If you struggle with sharing your faith, God can make you both willing and able. Consider this wonderful promise—*"For it is God which worketh in you both to will and to do of his good pleasure"* (Philippians 2:13). The Lord wants to help us! Ask Him to do so. The fact that you have started reading this book proves that He has already begun to work in your heart to become a better witness. Praise God for that!

If you are like me, you want people to be saved. I enjoy sharing the gospel with the lost, especially to those who have a desire to hear it. However, not everybody is receptive to the good news, and that can make it more difficult to witness. Whether you feel intimidated or inadequate, you can become more

Simple Soulwinning Steps

confident as a witness. I have discovered that people are more willing to share their faith when they know how to do it. That's why I wrote this book.

Simple Soulwinning Steps provides all that you need to know to get started. You will be challenged to see the condition of the lost and develop a burden for them. Then, you will discover many promises for soulwinners and realize that God not only goes with us but also works through us to win souls. Therefore, we have nothing to fear! Many other practical tips are presented in the pages that follow. They include: how to memorize key verses, how to witness to religious and non-religious people, how to handle objections, what to include in a soulwinning presentation, how to know if people are ready to be saved, and how to begin discipleship with new converts.

If your biggest hindrance to winning souls has been not knowing what to do, that is about to change! Get ready to take some simple soulwinning steps.

INTRODUCTION

How to Use This Book

Simple Soulwinning Steps provides practical tips that will equip you to share your faith. It can be used for personal study or as a soulwinning course in a church setting. In either case, if you follow the steps laid out in the following pages, you will be amazed at how the Lord can use you to spread the gospel!

The book is divided into two parts: *What to Do* and *What to Say*. In the first part, we will consider how to prepare our hearts and minds to win souls. In the second part, we will cover the main points that should be included in a soulwinning presentation.

Used as a Course at Church

This book can be used in conjunction with the *Simple Soulwinning Steps Workbook* and the *Simple Soulwinning Steps Course CDs*. The course has two levels: Beginner and Advanced. The requirements for reaching each level are listed in the *Simple Soulwinning Steps Workbook*.

Each week, you will be challenged to complete several assignments on your own. Additionally, you will recite memory verses to an accountability partner. By

Simple Soulwinning Steps

memorizing key verses from each lesson, you will be more prepared to evangelize the lost.

Depending on which level you choose to work on, you should expect to study between 1-2 hours per week to finish the requirements. If you get behind in any of your assignments, do your best to make them up the next week. Strive to complete all of the assignments in a timely manner.

If this course is being taken through a church program, we recommend that a certificate should be awarded to all who complete the course. If you are a slow learner, do not worry! The Lord will bless your desire to serve Him by helping you along the way. Remember that the goal of this course is to win souls, not merely to earn a certificate.

Used for Personal Study

You can learn how to win souls even without a church-wide course. Simply study the content of each lesson and put it into practice by looking for opportunities to witness in your daily life. As important as book knowledge is, it is also vital to get on-the-job training. This can be accomplished by going soulwinning with an experienced soulwinner. If your church has a soulwinning program, I recommend that you participate in it regularly.

Introduction

Learning the memory verses is a vital part of winning souls. So, I suggest that you ask someone in your family or church to listen to you as you recite verses each week. This will keep you accountable to learn God's Word.

Once you have completed this book, your confidence will increase because you'll know the basics of sharing the good news with others!

Part One

What to Do

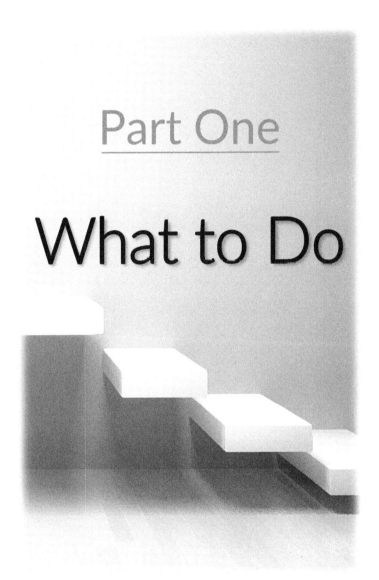

LESSON ONE

Stop and Think

Our thoughts determine our steps. When it comes to winning souls, we should seriously consider what we are doing. Solomon gave some good advice about thinking before doing. He said, *"Ponder the path of thy feet, and let all thy ways be established"* (Proverbs 4:26). By reflecting on key aspects of soulwinning, we will be better equipped for the task.

When considering a path, our main concern is where it will take us. As long as it brings us where we want to go, we are usually willing to put up with a few inconveniences along the way. The path of the soulwinner is not always easy. Many who take steps to reach the lost either get distracted or discouraged. That is why it is important to continually remind ourselves that the rewards at the end of the path are well worth the effort. Christ's lesson about the lost sheep illustrates this well. Though the man in the parable had to search diligently in the wilderness for the sheep, *"when he hath found it, he layeth it on his shoulders, rejoicing"* (Luke 15:5). Happiness awaits the Christian who faithfully seeks sinners. Rescuing lost souls not only brings joy to the soulwinner, but it also causes rejoicing in Heaven. Jesus said, *"I say unto you, that likewise joy shall be in heaven over one sinner that repenteth"* (Luke 15:7). There is joy on earth below and in Heaven above when a sinner gets saved! This should motivate us to take some steps to win souls to Christ.

Let's take a few moments to contemplate the plight of the lost through the eyes of the Lord. When we see as He sees, we will begin to think as He thinks. And as we already mentioned, that will lead us to take steps that He would have us take—soulwinning steps. Consider three things that will compel you to win souls: the concern of the Lord, the condition of the lost, and the consequences of lingering.

The Concern of the Lord

If you want to know what is important to someone, consider what he talks about, what he spends his time doing, and what he is willing to sacrifice for. By observing the life of Jesus, it is obvious that He has always been concerned about lost souls. He spoke much about reaching the unsaved, He actively pursued them, and He sacrificed His life for them. In fact, Christ's main purpose on earth was to save sinners—*"For the Son of man is come to seek and to save that which was lost"* (Luke 19:10). Aren't you glad that Jesus sought you? Well, He cares about every unsaved person in the world as much as He cares about you and wants them to

Stop and Think

be saved too. Let's ponder Christ's concern for the lost and see how it ought to motivate us to win souls.

To get a good glimpse into the heart of Jesus, we simply need to study Matthew 9:35-38. As you read these familiar verses, notice how He longed to help the people, not merely physically but also spiritually.

"And Jesus went about all the cities and villages, teaching in their synagogues, and preaching the gospel of the kingdom, and healing every sickness and every disease among the people. But when he saw the multitudes, he was moved with compassion on them, because they fainted, and were scattered abroad, as sheep having no shepherd. Then saith he unto his disciples, The harvest truly is plenteous, but the labourers are few; Pray ye therefore the Lord of the harvest, that he will send forth labourers into his harvest" (Matthew 9:35-38).

In the above passage, we see five elements of true concern for the lost. Notice that Christ-like concern is more than an attitude. It involves action.

First, true concern causes us to go. Jesus did not wait for people to come to Him. He deliberately set out to bring the gospel to others—*"And Jesus went about all the cities and villages, teaching...and preaching."* If you lack concern for the lost, the way to develop a burden is

Simple Soulwinning Steps

to go and witness to someone. As you interact with the unsaved and discuss spiritual matters with them, you will see how badly they need the Lord. So, whether you feel like it or not, go! You will be glad that you did.

Second, true concern causes us to see. Notice what happened after Jesus went teaching and preaching— *"...he saw the multitudes."* Going leads to seeing. Christ saw the true condition of the people that He witnessed to. He commented that *"they fainted, and were scattered abroad, as sheep having no shepherd."* The word *faint* refers to losing strength or being dejected. Our world is filled with people who are weary of life because of the effects of sin. They are downhearted and discouraged. Jesus also noticed that the lost were scattered and without a shepherd. People are wandering aimlessly through life nearing the dangerous precipice of hell. They need someone to guide them to safety. The more we go after souls, the more we will see how much the world really needs the Lord.

Third, true concern causes us to feel. Although we should not be controlled by our emotions, we should not be unemotional. In fact, Christ expressed great emotion. After He saw the needs of the multitude, *"he was moved with compassion on them."* Compassion involves sorrow and sympathy. When Jesus considered the spiritual condition of the people, His heart was filled with pain and pity. It bothered Him to see people needlessly suffering in their sin. Paul expressed a similar burden for the lost, saying, *"I have great heaviness and continual sorrow in my heart"* (Romans 9:2). Do you have deep feelings for the lost? Instead of seeking a life of comfort and ease, we should be willing to carry a burden for those without Christ. If we do, we will be rewarded with great joy when they turn to the Savior.

Fourth, true concern causes us to move. Biblical compassion does not stop with mere feelings. It leads to involvement. When speaking about reaching the lost, David Livingstone aptly said, "Sympathy is no substitute for action." Jesus was *"moved with compassion."* He did more than see the need and say, "Oh, it is too bad that those poor people have no shepherd." He did something about it! In Mark's Gospel, we see another time that Jesus was moved with compassion. After seeing the people *"as sheep not having a shepherd,"* Christ took action—*"...he began to teach them many things"* (Mark 6:34).

Notice also from Matthew 9 that Jesus pointed out the need to His disciples, saying, *"The harvest truly is plenteous, but the labourers are few."* It is not enough to get involved in the harvest. We must also compel others to do the same.

Fifth, true concern causes us to pray. Great needs require great prayer. Jesus did not want the disciples to forget about what they had seen. Therefore, He compelled them, *"Pray ye therefore the Lord of the harvest, that he will send forth labourers into his*

Simple Soulwinning Steps

harvest." If we fail to pray for the lost, it reveals a lack of concern for them. We ought to beg God to send more soulwinners to reach the fainting multitudes. As we do, we will be stirred to get involved in the harvest too.

Jesus was so concerned about the lost that He trained and sent His disciples to reach them. *"Then said Jesus to them again, Peace be unto you: as my Father hath sent me, even so send I you"* (John 20:21). If we claim to be disciples, then His message to us is the same—*"so send I you."* God's plan to reach the world is for His people to share the good news with everyone. Christ said, *"Go ye into all the world, and preach the gospel to every creature"* (Mark 16:15). If every Christian obeyed this simple command, the world would soon be evangelized. Since seeking the lost is important to Jesus, it ought to be to us too.

The Condition of the Lost

Despite the façade, many people in the world are more miserable than they appear. They spend a great deal of time pretending to be happy, but they have no true joy within. Solomon spoke of this, saying, *"Even in laughter the heart is sorrowful; and the end of that mirth is heaviness"* (Proverbs 14:13). No matter how hard people try to mask their feelings, the Bible reveals their true condition. By realizing the state of unbelievers, you

Stop and Think

will be able to look past the veneer and realize that they are in desperate need of help. Notice what God says about the unsaved.

First, they wander. The prophet Isaiah likened mankind to wayward sheep. He said, *"All we like sheep have gone astray; we have turned every one to his own way"* (Isaiah 53:6). Because of their sin, lost folks are far from the Shepherd, which leaves them with no one to care for their needs. Jesus is the Good Shepherd. He nourishes, leads, and protects His sheep. Those without Christ lack all of that. It is our duty to seek the lost as sheep who have wandered from their shepherd, knowing that they will be much better off once we get them to Jesus. Let each of us *"go after that which is lost, until he find it"* (Luke 15:4).

Second, they are lost. The lost condition of mankind is so terrible that Jesus was compelled to leave Heaven to provide a remedy—*"For the Son of man is come to seek and to save that which was lost"* (Luke 19:10). We often refer to people without Christ as being lost. However, many tend to overlook what it means to be lost. The Greek word for *lost* is also translated in verb form as *perish* in John 3:16. To be lost literally refers to those who will perish and suffer eternal destruction. Rather than flippantly refer to people as hopelessly lost, let us see their condition as dire.

Third, they are in darkness. Darkness is the absence of light. It produces uncertainty, fear, and stumbling.

Simple Soulwinning Steps

Spiritual darkness is much the same way—*"The way of the wicked is as darkness: they know not at what they stumble"* (Proverbs 4:19). Without Christ, people are prone to falter and fall, which leads to a life of frustration. We should never think that sinners truly enjoy the results of living in darkness. What they need is someone to lead them to the Light of the World so that He can dispel the darkness in their souls. Jesus came to *"give light to them that sit in darkness and in the shadow of death"* (Luke 1:79). We must take *"the light of the glorious gospel of Christ"* to them (2 Corinthians 4:4). Further, we are commanded, *"Let your light so shine before men, that they may see your good works, and glorify your Father which is in heaven"* (Matthew 5:16). How bright is your light to those around you? Are you radiating the love of Christ and sharing the light of the gospel with others?

Fourth, they are blind. Unfortunately, many lost people cannot see their true condition. The Lord tells us why—*"...the god of this world* [the devil] *hath blinded the minds of them which believe not, lest the light of the glorious gospel of Christ, who is the image of God, should shine unto them"* (2 Corinthians 4:4). Satan distorts the truth and deceives people. The song *Amazing Grace* records John Newton's testimony. He penned, "I once was lost, was blind, but now I see." Oh, how the lost will see life differently after receiving Christ!

Stop and Think

Fifth, they have no peace. The world is full of turmoil, and people carry heavy burdens. They often turn everywhere but to God for help. To make matters worse, sin prevents them from having a relationship with the Lord. Although sin promises them a good time, it brings the opposite. Sin offers freedom, but it leads to enslavement. It boasts of pleasure but ends in misery. People may love their sin, but they are not fond of its consequences. God assures us that they lack peace— *"There is no peace, saith the LORD, unto the wicked"* (Isaiah 48:22). Regardless of how happy sinners may look outwardly, we know that their soul is not satisfied. Sin is a thief. It robs its victim of rest and tranquility, making them miserable. Lost souls need to be introduced to Jesus, the Prince of Peace. Notice what God promises to the saved—*"Peace I leave with you, my peace I give unto you"* (John 14:27). Let us not hesitate to offer the message of peace to those who have none.

Sixth, they carry guilt. Every lost sinner is guilty in the eyes of God because of his disobedience. *"For whosoever shall keep the whole law, and yet offend in one point, he is guilty of all"* (James 2:10). Though *"he is guilty"* of breaking God's Law, he may not feel the full weight of that guilt until the Holy Spirit arrests his conscience with the Word of God. That is why we must faithfully present God's Word to the lost. Thankfully, we not only have a message that brings conviction but it

Simple Soulwinning Steps

also provides hope. We can tell others that God offers a full pardon!

The truth is that many people struggle with guilt more than we realize. I recall witnessing to a neighbor who was a faithful Catholic. She was diagnosed with cancer and was admitted to the hospital. When I visited her, the Lord gave me a wonderful opportunity to share the plan of salvation with her. That night she received Christ as her Savior. After she prayed to be saved, she made a comment that revealed the unseen battle with guilt she had been experiencing. She said, "I didn't know what I was going to do with all of my sin." Even though she was kind and religious, she knew in her heart that she was guilty before God. There are more people in the world just like her, and it is our job to reach them before it is too late!

Seventh, they are condemned. When a man is condemned, he is pronounced guilty and doomed to suffer punishment. We don't like to think about judgment, but we must not forget the awful fate awaiting unbelievers. Jesus said, *"He that believeth on him is not condemned: but he that believeth not is condemned already, because he hath not believed in the name of the only begotten Son of God"* (John 3:18). A lost sinner lives precariously, dangling over eternal flames as if by a thread. We must compassionately warn them of pending danger and urge them to trust the Savior before it is too late.

Eighth, they are spiritually dead. Mankind is composed of body, soul, and spirit. People can be alive physically but dead spiritually. Paul mentioned that salvation brings spiritual life to soul—*"And you hath he quickened, who were dead in trespasses and sins"* (Ephesians 2:1). As Christians, we must learn to see people not just as physical beings. Too often we interact with others and forget that they have an eternal soul. It would help greatly if we could envision lost people as alive physically but dead spiritually. Thankfully, Christ gives life!

Ninth, they are without hope. Most people want to go to Heaven when they die, but those without Jesus have no hope of eternal life. When Paul addressed the believers in Ephesus, he described their condition before salvation—*"That at that time ye were without Christ...having no hope, and without God in the world"* (Ephesians 2:12). The words *"no hope"* are sobering. The lost have no hope in this life. We see people all around us who are filled with fear, anxiety, and discouragement. What they need is a relationship with *"the God of hope"* Who can fill them *"with all joy and peace in believing"* (Romans 15:13).

Not only do the unsaved have no hope in this life, they will have no hope throughout eternity. All who fail to receive Jesus as their Savior before they die will get no second chance. Their eternity is set once they exhale

Simple Soulwinning Steps

their last breath. Let us bring them the message of hope before they become eternally hopeless.

Tenth, they are destined for eternal punishment. Some of the most sobering words in the Bible describe the final judgment of the lost, who will join Satan in eternal flames. *"And whosoever was not found written in the book of life was cast into the lake of fire"* (Revelation 20:15). How is such suffering described? The Bible says that those who are *"cast into the lake of fire and brimstone...shall be tormented day and night for ever and ever"* (Revelation 20:10). If you have ever experienced a minor burn, you probably remember how painful it was. People in burn units at a hospital suffer excruciating pain. A slight touch or gentle breeze can be seemingly unbearable in some cases. No earthly pain can rival the unending torment awaiting the lost. Few of us like to think much about the suffering that will be experienced in hell and the lake of fire, but God does not want us to forget how terrible it is. Though He loves sinners, he has to punish sin. *"Knowing therefore the terror of the Lord, we persuade men"* (2 Corinthians 5:11). Allow the fate of the lost to disturb you enough to tell them the good news of Christ.

Now that we have considered the condition of the lost, I hope you realize that people may be hungrier for spiritual instruction than you first thought. They wander through life aimlessly and have no peace. They are blind and stumble in darkness. They carry a load of guilt and have no hope. Surely, the good news of the gospel can completely change their condition! Let this build your confidence in striking up a conversation with a lost sinner.

The Consequences of Lingering

Jesus referred to lost souls as a waiting harvest which needed to be reaped in a timely manner. When the disciples apparently made excuses in their hearts for not reaching the lost in Samaria, Jesus corrected them. He said, *"Say not ye, There are yet four months, and then cometh harvest? behold, I say unto you, Lift up your eyes, and look on the fields; for they are white already to harvest"* (John 4:35). If a field is not harvested when it is ready, the harvest will eventually rot. In other words, the harvest will be missed. People do not wait for us to tell them about Christ before they die. If we miss the opportunity to bring them to Jesus, they will be lost forever.

Jesus further said, *"The harvest truly is great, but the labourers are few: pray ye therefore the Lord of the harvest, that he would send forth labourers into his harvest"* (Luke 10:2). Christ indicated that the workload is bigger than the workforce. In other words, there are more souls to be reached than there are soulwinners to reach them. The obvious solution is to send more laborers into the harvest fields. However, what happens

Simple Soulwinning Steps

if the laborers do not go? A harvest that is not reaped when it is ready will eventually rot. Let us not be responsible for one waiting soul to miss eternity in Heaven.

Think of the harvest as people who are ready to be saved. What will happen to them if nobody brings the gospel to them? They will die without Christ and spend eternity *"in the lake which burneth with fire and brimstone: which is the second death"* (Revelation 21:8). John Wesley's words should sober us all. He said, "Untold millions are still untold." Hasn't Christ commissioned us to tell them? Why have they not been told? Christians have become distracted by things that do not have eternal value. We allow worldliness, apathy, and fear to cause us to neglect the harvest. Paul confronted the believers in Corinth for not actively seeking the lost. He said, *"Awake to righteousness, and sin not; for some have not the knowledge of God: I speak this to your shame"* (1 Corinthians 15:34). It is as if Paul said, "Shame on you that there are people who haven't heard the gospel!" Have you been sleeping during harvest time? If so, it's time to wake up and start sharing your faith.

The prophet Jeremiah lamented the fate of the Jews in Jerusalem who would fail to be delivered. He cried out, *"The harvest is past, the summer is ended, and we are not saved"* (Jeremiah 8:20). I wonder how many lost souls of our day will cry out in eternity, *"The harvest is past...and we are not saved."* If we miss the waiting harvest, the consequences are awful and eternal.

Conclusion

We must learn to see lost souls as God sees them. When we realize their true condition, our compassion will increase and so will our confidence in the message of the gospel. Jesus came to seek the lost, and we must follow His example. Let's stop making excuses for not entering the fields, and begin to reap the waiting harvest.

Pause and consider the plight of the lost. The only proven remedy for sin-sick souls is Jesus. Allow this truth to motivate you to point people to the Great Physician. He is ready to cleanse, heal, and renew every repentant sinner.

LESSON TWO

Get Ready

Winning souls begins with preparation. The apostle Paul said, *"So, as much as in me is, I am ready to preach the gospel"* (Romans 1:15). He was ready because he took time to prepare. Perhaps that is why God used him as greatly as He did. If we want to be successful at winning souls, we should get ourselves in a state of readiness. Here are a few simple ideas to help you prepare spiritually, physically, and mentally.

Spiritual Preparation

To prepare our hearts, we must do two main things: pray and depend upon the Holy Spirit.

First, pray. Always begin with real, heartfelt prayer. Remember, that you can do little to persuade sinners in your own strength; you need God's help to do God's business! What should you ask in prayer?

1. <u>Ask for wisdom.</u> None of us knows exactly what kind of questions or reactions we will encounter while out soulwinning. Instead of worrying about the unknown, we should pray about it. Here's a wonderful promise to claim—*"If any of*

Simple Soulwinning Steps

you lack wisdom, let him ask of God, that giveth to all men liberally, and upbraideth not; and it shall be given him" (James 1:5). The Lord will help you to know what to say and how to say it if you ask Him.

2. <u>Ask for power</u>. We cannot win people to Christ with our oratory skills. We must trust the Lord to speak to hearts through His Word. Thankfully, God has promised to empower our witness. Jesus said, *"But ye shall receive power, after that the Holy Ghost is come upon you: and ye shall be witnesses unto me both in Jerusalem, and in all Judaea, and in Samaria, and unto the uttermost part of the earth"* (Acts 1:8). Through the Holy Spirit, we can be *"endued with power from on high"* (Luke 24:49). Since we are promised this power, we can confidently ask for it before we go out witnessing.

3. <u>Ask for boldness</u>. Some people are shyer than others, but even great men of faith like Paul sought boldness through prayer. Consider one of his prayer requests, *"And for me, that utterance may be given unto me, that I may open my mouth boldly, to make known the mystery of the gospel"* (Ephesians 6:19). If you struggle with being timid, you can pray like the apostles did. "And when they had prayed, the place was

shaken where they were assembled together; and they were all filled with the Holy Ghost, and they spake the word of God with boldness" (Acts 4:31). How reassuring it is to know that when we pray for boldness, God will give it to us!

4. <u>Ask for peace</u>. God does not want us to become uptight, anxious, or fearful about witnessing. Such attitudes may be common, but they are not honoring to the Lord. Here is another great promise to remember when serving the Lord, *"For God hath not given us the spirit of fear; but of power, and of love, and of a sound mind"* (2 Timothy 1:7). We can enjoy the peace of God when doing His will. Don't forget to ask for it.

5. <u>Ask for protection</u>. It is comforting to know that when we go out witnessing, the Lord is with us. Jesus said, *"Go ye therefore, and teach all nations, baptizing them in the name of the Father, and of the Son, and of the Holy Ghost: Teaching them to observe all things whatsoever I have commanded you: and, lo, I am with you alway, even unto the end of the world. Amen"* (Matthew 28:19-20). The words *"I am with you alway"* are very precious! What have we to fear when He is near? With confidence we can ask for God's protection.

Simple Soulwinning Steps

6. <u>Ask for guidance</u>. Not only does the Lord promise to go *with* us, He also promises to go *before* us. Moses experienced this truth. He said, *"And the LORD, he it is that doth go before thee; he will be with thee, he will not fail thee, neither forsake thee: fear not, neither be dismayed"* (Deuteronomy 31:8). God can guide our steps and lead us to people who need His Word. Not only that, but He will guide us to know what to say. Jesus said, *"Howbeit when he, the Spirit of truth, is come, he will guide you into all truth"* (John 16:13). Let's be certain to ask for God's leading when we witness for Him, knowing that He will keep His promise.

7. <u>Ask for results</u>. We should expect the Lord to do something when we share His Word with others. Not everybody who hears the gospel will get saved, but some will. Paul asked God to save sinners. He said, *"Brethren, my heart's desire and prayer to God for Israel is, that they might be saved"* (Romans 10:1). Let us follow his example and ask the Lord to work in the hearts of those we witness to. When Jesus spoke to Peter about reaching the lost, He promised some success— *"Fear not; from henceforth thou shalt catch men"* (Luke 5:10). Although none of us is promised how many souls will be saved, the promise *"thou*

shalt catch men" is quite encouraging. So, let us ask God to bless our evangelism efforts.

Jesus tied together the idea of winning souls and prayer. He said, *"I have chosen you, and ordained you, that ye should go and bring forth fruit...that whatsoever ye shall ask of the Father in my name, he may give it you"* (John 15:16). Since He has chosen us to bear fruit and promises to give what we ask, let's be sure to ask for souls to be saved. If we learn to consistently ask the Lord for help in our soulwinning efforts, He will answer because He wants souls to be saved even more than we do!

Second, depend upon the Holy Spirit. Witnessing to others requires supernatural assistance. We are not capable of influencing a person's heart, but God can. In particular, the ministry of the Holy Spirit is to bring conviction when we present the Word of God to others. Jesus said, *"And when he is come, he will reprove the world of sin, and of righteousness, and of judgment"* (John 16:8).

Notice how the Holy Spirit can help us as we witness to others:

1. <u>He enables</u>. If you feel inadequate or unqualified to tell others about salvation, you are not alone. Thankfully, the Spirit empowers us. *"But ye shall receive power, after that the Holy Ghost is come upon you: and ye shall be*

witnesses unto me both in Jerusalem, and in all Judaea, and in Samaria, and unto the uttermost part of the earth" (Acts 1:8). He gives us the ability to witness effectively. Though we may not be confident in ourselves, we can trust God to make us *"able ministers of the new testament"* (2 Corinthians 3:6).

2. <u>He reminds us which Bible verses to use</u>. Are you ever at a loss for words? The Holy Spirit will help us to remember portions of God's Word so we can share it with others. *"But the Comforter, which is the Holy Ghost, whom the Father will send in my name, he shall teach you all things, and bring all things to your remembrance, whatsoever I have said unto you"* (John 14:26). The more familiar you become with the Bible, the more Scriptures the Spirit can help you to recall. That is why it is important to hide God's Word in our hearts.

3. <u>He guides you what to say</u>. We are not alone when we are witnessing. God's Spirit is right there to remind us what to say next. *"Howbeit when he, the Spirit of truth, is come, he will guide you into all truth: for he shall not speak of himself; but whatsoever he shall hear, that shall he speak: and he will shew you things to come"* (John 16:13). Since no two people have the

Get Ready

same exact needs, the Holy Spirit will guide you to share just the right verses with each person.

4. <u>He directs us to people who need to be saved</u>. Consider some examples of how the Holy Spirit guided Christians to witness to the lost. First, He led Philip to the Ethiopian man in the desert— *"Then the Spirit said unto Philip, Go near, and join thyself to this chariot. And Philip ran thither to him, and heard him read the prophet Esaias, and said, Understandest thou what thou readest?"* (Acts 8:29-30). Philip was able to share the gospel with a man who was seeking to worship God. There are people who want to know God but lack someone to teach them. Second, God sent Peter to witness to Cornelius, the Gentile centurion. He also was a lost man who was seeking the Lord. Consider how God led Peter. *"While Peter thought on the vision, the Spirit said unto him, Behold, three men seek thee. Arise therefore, and get thee down, and go with them, doubting nothing: for I have sent them"* (Acts 10:19-20). The Spirit made it quite clear that he was to speak to Cornelius. When Peter rehearsed the matter to the apostles, he said, *"And the Spirit bade me go with them, nothing doubting"* (Acts 11:12). Don't miss the wording—*"the Spirit bade me go."* At times,

Simple Soulwinning Steps

God's Spirit will nudge us to speak to the lost. We must be sensitive to His leading so that we don't miss an opportunity to help a seeking sinner.

5. <u>He helps our weaknesses</u>. Perhaps you feel like you are not very eloquent or highly educated. Don't worry about what you lack because the Holy Spirit can make up for your deficiencies. Paul gave some encouraging words—*"Likewise the Spirit also helpeth our infirmities"* (Romans 8:26a). When God does mighty things through weak people, He gets more glory! So, learn to look at your weakness as an asset, knowing that it makes you a prime candidate to receive God's help! Simply make yourself available for the Lord to use and trust His Spirit to help bolster you to get the job done.

6. <u>He prays for us</u>. Even though we are prone to fail, we have One praying for us Who can never fail—*"...for we know not what we should pray for as we ought: but the Spirit itself maketh intercession for us with groanings which cannot be uttered"* (Romans 8:26b). Knowing that the Holy Spirit intercedes on our behalf brings great reassurance. Our confidence tends to increase when we know that our friends are praying for us. If we gain comfort from their prayers,

Get Ready

shouldn't we consider the Spirit's prayers even more effective? Praise God for the undergirding prayer of the Holy Spirit!

7. <u>He overcomes our fear</u>. It is natural to fear. That is why the Lord repeatedly tells us throughout the Bible, *"Fear not."* Because we have the Holy Spirit, we have no need to fear. Consider what Paul said, *"For ye have not received the spirit of bondage again to fear; but ye have received the Spirit of adoption, whereby we cry, Abba, Father"* (Romans 8:15). The Holy Spirt enables us to cry out to our Heavenly Father. No loving father would abandon his child in time of difficulty, and God will not leave us to fend for ourselves. Face your fear of witnessing by enlisting help from the Lord.

8. <u>He convinces the lost</u>. It takes a lot of pressure off the soulwinner when he realizes that it is not his job to convince people to be saved. When speaking of the Holy Spirit, Jesus said, *"And when he is come, he will reprove the world of sin, and of righteousness, and of judgment"* (John 16:8). The word *reprove* means "to convict; to convince." The Spirit of God uses the Word of God to produce conviction in the hearts of mankind, convincing them not only of their sin but also of their need for Christ. We should

never force anyone to make a decision. We must simply present the truth and allow God to work in hearts. Sometimes people resist and fight against God's conviction. No person will ever get saved because you present a clever, convincing argument. Allow the Spirit to do His job in hearts. When people submit and respond to His conviction, you will be able to lead them to Christ.

Hopefully, the reasons listed above will motivate you to seek the Holy Spirit's help in your soulwinning efforts. He promises to do for us what we cannot do in our own strength. He wants to work through us. Knowing this should encourage you that, with God's help, you can witness for Him!

Now that we have considered preparing spiritually through prayer and dependence upon the Holy Spirit, let us turn our attention to another matter.

Physical Preparation

A farmer who goes to the field does not go empty-handed, and a soulwinner who goes to the harvest of souls must have his tools ready also! How should you prepare yourself?

First, take a Bible or New Testament with you. People need God's Word in order to be saved. Peter reminds us of this necessity, saying, *"Being born again,*

Get Ready

not of corruptible seed, but of incorruptible, by the word of God, which liveth and abideth for ever" (1 Peter 1:23). The Word of God is likened to a seed. It must be sown in a heart before eternal life is produced. A soulwinner simply cannot do his job without the Scriptures. At times you may have to witness using verses from memory, but you can be more effective by having many verses at your disposal. Additionally, when people can see for themselves the truth written in the Bible, it lends credibility to your message.

Second, dress appropriately. When you go out to win souls, you represent the King of kings. Paul said, *"Now then we are ambassadors for Christ"* (2 Corinthians 5:20). As ambassadors, we should not be disheveled and unkempt when we participate in our church's soulwinning program. I'm not suggesting that we have to wear expensive clothing or adorn ourselves in the latest fashions. We should be clean, look sharp, and act properly. Of course, there will be situations when we might not look our best, but we can still witness. For example, a construction worker on his way home from work can certainly give out a tract to someone he meets at a gas station, bank, or grocery store because it is obvious he has been working.

Third, use gospel tracts. A warm smile, kind word, and display of confidence in your personal faith will make a big difference in how tracts are received. A good tract contains a clear presentation of the gospel that can

Simple Soulwinning Steps

be read even after your visit is over. In fact, many people in one home might read the same tract! Even if you do not get to present the gospel to someone, always try to leave a tract. It can continue working after your conversation is over. When promoting the use of tracts, Charles Spurgeon said, "There is a real service of Christ in the distribution of the gospel in its printed form, a service the result of which heaven alone shall disclose, and the judgment day alone discover. How many thousands have been carried to heaven instrumentally upon the wings of these tracts, none can tell."[1]

Fourth, carry a pen and paper. You may need to record a person's name, address, or phone number to contact him later. If you are canvassing a street, it is helpful to indicate the responses you get at each home. This is especially helpful when returning to a street to knock on doors where you did not get an answer. Another reason to carry a pen and paper is so that you can write down Scripture references to leave with individuals who may want to study a topic in more detail. As you can see, it is always good to be equipped.

Fifth, bring helpful resources with you. The charts and verse references in this book can greatly assist your witness. Therefore, they have been condensed and included in Appendix A, which can be detached and kept

---

[1] https://www.azquotes.com/quote/1203773, accessed on 11/1/2020.

in your Bible for quick reference. Don't be afraid to refer to it if you need help while sharing the gospel.

Sixth, schedule a regular time to go soulwinning. Do not let other things interfere with your commitment to win souls. Since the devil does not want people to hear about Jesus, you can be certain that he will try to get you sidetracked. Be faithful, be focused, and be determined to spread the good news!

We have seen the importance to prepare spiritually and physically. Now let us turn our attention to making sure that we have the right attitude when soulwinning.

Mental Preparation

It is important to remember your goal when witnessing to others. You are not out to win an argument; you are trying to win a soul. Too often, conversations between a Christian and lost people end in an argument, and that is not spiritual. If you belligerently strive to make your point, you will get nowhere. You should not argue in the flesh. Witnessing is a spiritual matter, and you must prepare yourself mentally to stay on track. Consider how God wants us to witness.

First, be compassionate. *"And of some have compassion, making a difference"* (Jude 22). Love can make a huge difference. There are many people in the world who are hurting. They think that no one seems to notice them or to care about their needs. When people know that you are concerned for them, they are more likely to respond to your message.

Second, be gracious. The soulwinner must always be kind and courteous. *"Let your speech be alway with grace, seasoned with salt, that ye may know how ye ought to answer every man"* (Colossians 4:6). Even when we meet opposition, we must show great restraint and speak *"with grace."*

Third, be humble. Nobody likes a know-it-all. As Christ was meek, we should be too. Peter reminds us, *"But sanctify the Lord God in your hearts: and be ready always to give an answer to every man that asketh you a reason of the hope that is in you with meekness and fear"* (1 Peter 3:15). A proud soulwinner pushes people away, but a humble one draws people to Christ. Rather than boast about how good you are or how much you know about the Bible, give God the glory for what He has done in your life. When pride takes a backseat, people will see Christ, not you.

Fourth, be gentle. There are enough harsh people in the world already. Paul reminded us how we should approach people—*"And the servant of the Lord must not strive; but be gentle unto all men, apt to teach, patient, In meekness instructing those that oppose themselves; if God peradventure will give them repentance to the acknowledging of the truth; And that they may recover themselves out of the snare of the devil, who are taken* captive by him at his will" (2 Timothy 2:24-26). Do not get upset when people resist you. As this passage states, they *"oppose themselves"* too. We can expect some rough responses by the lost, but we must remain even-tempered. A gentle spirit can help deliver someone from *"the snare of the devil."*

Fifth, be patient. Read 2 Timothy 2:24 again. Notice the word *patient*. Don't get angry or frustrated at people when they fail to understand the Bible. Some people have to hear the gospel several times before they fully understand. Be satisfied with gaining small victories along the way.

Conclusion

If you begin to see unsaved people as lost souls that Christ died to save, you will approach them in the right way. Do not respond in a fleshly manner, even if they are rude. Allow the Holy Spirit to control you, and you will make a great impact as they see *"Christ in you"* (Colossians 1:27).

LESSON THREE

Follow God's Plan

We have looked in detail at how to get ready to win souls. Praise God that He equips us spiritually, physically, and mentally! But what's next? What is God's plan to reach the lost? It's quite simple.

Go!

After you have prayed and prepared, GO! It is time to put feet to your faith. What good does it do to prepare to win souls but not go out and try to win them? Consider the words of Jesus to His disciples:

> *"Go ye into all the world, and preach the gospel to every creature"* (Mark 16:15).
>
> *"Go ye therefore, and teach all nations"* (Matthew 28:19).
>
> *"Peace be unto you: as my Father hath sent me, even so send I you"* (John 20:21).
>
> *"...repentance and remission of sins should be preached in his name among all nations"* (Luke 24:47).

Simple Soulwinning Steps

Clearly, Christ wants us to get busy and look for some people with whom we can share the good news. The command is, *"Go."* That involves action and direction. We cannot passively wait for people to approach us. We can *go* down the street to see a neighbor, *go* across town on visitation, *go* to a loved one's home, or *go* out of our way to give a stranger a gospel tract. Years ago, my pastor made a statement that stuck with me. He said, "The only alternative to soulwinning is disobedience." To delay is to disobey.

A good way to learn how to witness is to observe an experienced soulwinner at work. If your church has a soulwinning outreach, determine to be there the next time it meets. Ask to be put with someone who knows how to witness and watch what they do. If your schedule absolutely does not allow you to make it for the church's soulwinning program, there may be someone else in the same predicament who would be willing to go with you at a different time. Try your best to find a soulwinning partner who you can regularly visit with. Most pastors would be happy to help you find a partner. By making visitation part of your weekly schedule, you will learn to become a faithful soulwinner.

Sharing the good news with the lost should not be something that you limit to once a week during church visitation. You should look for opportunities to witness in your daily life. Most of us come in contact with lost people just about every day. You can hand out tracts

Follow God's Plan

and try to strike up conversations with friends, relatives, neighbors, coworkers, business contacts, bank tellers, store clerks, and many more. When encouraging the use of gospel tracts, Charles Spurgeon said, "Let each one of us, if we have done nothing for Christ, begin to do something now. The distribution of tracts is the first thing."[2] Take a step and go tell someone about the Savior. The Lord will help you.

Say Something!

As we have indicated, going out to reach the lost is more than making social visits. Jesus said, *"And as ye go, preach"* (Matthew 10:7). The word *preach* refers to proclaiming and publishing the good news of salvation. All Christians are responsible to open their mouths and tell people about Jesus. That sounds simple, but how do we get started? Sometimes it can seem difficult to change the subject to spiritual matters. Consider how to transition to the gospel in the following scenarios.

Witnessing Door to Door

When going door to door soulwinning, it is usually much easier to begin talking about the Bible because people figure that is why you are there. Here are a few tips you can follow.

---

[2] https://www.azquotes.com/quote/866705, accessed on 11/1/2020.

Simple Soulwinning Steps

1. Introduce yourself and your partner. Be warm and friendly. Remember that you are a stranger. So, try to put them at ease. Be genuine and sincere—not phony or fearful!

2. Tell them what you are doing and where you are from. Most people get suspicious when strangers beat around the bush. Openness builds trust.

3. Hand them some gospel literature and ask them if they have a church they attend regularly. If they do, they will usually tell you which one. This does a couple of things. First, it allows you find out their religious background, which will help you to know how to witness to them. Second, if someone does not attend church, you can invite them to visit your church.

4. Unless someone is really interested in your church, don't spend too much time talking about your church. You may have the greatest church in the world with modern facilities and great programs, but most lost people are not very interested in church. Besides, if you make the conversation only about your church, they may simply end the conversation by saying, "Thanks, but we already have a church." Focus on God's

Follow God's Plan

love and forgiveness more than on buildings and programs.

5. Try to transition the conversation to the topic of salvation. Either hand the person a gospel tract or point to the one you have already given them, and start talking about eternity. Here are a few suggestions to get started:

   - ✓ "This pamphlet discusses how to have a relationship with God and have eternal life."

   - ✓ "Most people want to go to Heaven when they die, but many are not sure how to get there. May I take a few minutes to show you how you can be sure of going to Heaven?"

   - ✓ "Let me ask you a question. If you died today, would you say that you are you 100%, 75%, or 50% sure that you will go to Heaven?"

   - ✓ "I used to be confused about how to go to Heaven, but someone showed me from the Bible how I could know for sure. May I show you what that shared with me?" [This is very effective because it involves your personal testimony.]

   - ✓ "You probably know that God has a wonderful plan for all of our lives. May I

Simple Soulwinning Steps

share with you from the Bible how you can begin that relationship with God?"

6. Stay on the subject of salvation. If someone asks a question about other topics in the Bible, you should say something like, "That is a good question, and I would be happy to discuss it later; however, let's finish talking about salvation first."

7. Hold your Bible so the person can see what you are sharing with them. It is important for people to see that your message is God's Word, not merely your ideas.

8. After you read a verse, explain what it means. Be sure to define words that are not common in today's English. When you have simple verses, try the following approach. Read the verse and ask the person what he/she thinks that God is trying to say. This involves the person in the conversation and gets him/her thinking. It also prevents people from thinking that you are only presenting your opinion.

What we just discussed will help you get the conversation started when going door to door. We will discuss more about what to include in your soulwinning presentation in later chapters. Now let's consider how to make the transition to spiritual matters in other situations.

Witnessing in Daily Life

Sharing the gospel in our day-to-day lives can be challenging, especially since many of our interactions with people are short. Using gospel tracts helps to break the ice. When meeting people at the gas station, bank, or grocery store, we usually only have enough time to hand someone a tract and quickly explain what's inside. I try to think of a way to introduce each tract I pass out. For example, I like to use a tract entitled *Amazing Grace: A True Story*. I typically say something like, "You probably have heard this song before, but in case you didn't know, there is a true story behind it." Many people will eagerly take the tract to find out more. If I have a little more time, I might say, "The song was written by a bad man after God changed his life. The same grace that changed him is available to help us too." Sometimes it opens the door for a more thorough witness. I have another tract that I like to use. The cover reads, "Times are tough. Look up!" When handing that tract to someone, I like to say, "With all the bad news in the world, here is some good news." I have had people thank me for giving them a message of hope. Then I can tell them that God has a wonderful plan for their lives and they can learn more about it in the tract.

Simple Soulwinning Steps

Tracts are great because they automatically turn your conversation to spiritual matters.

Sometimes, your interactions with people are extended and have nothing to do with the Bible. For instance, maybe you work in an office with someone and discuss business most of the day. Making the transition to talking about eternity can be difficult. It may take more work to make the transition to spiritual matters, but if you look for an opportunity, you should be able to steer the conversation to the things of God. For example, you can say something like, "The world sure is a mess these days." When the person agrees, you can add, "God warned us about this in the Bible." That is like putting bait on a fishing hook. You are hoping the person will nibble at it and ask what God says about the end times. The possibilities of how to turn a conversation to the Lord are endless. If you look for an opening, you will find a way to relate the Bible to current events in the world.

Occasionally, people will open up to you about their problems or fears. My father is getting up in years and needed me to take him to the doctor's office one day. When talking to the nurse, my dad commented that he had a good long life and was looking forward to Heaven because he would have a new body. The nurse responded, "I'm afraid to die." That was all that my dad needed to hear to turn the conversation to eternal life through Christ. She listened attentively for the next few

Follow God's Plan

minutes and my dad and I witnessed to her. Whether people have family problems, health problems, or emotional problems, the Bible has the answer. I have counseled unsaved couples because I knew it would give me an opportunity to explain their most important need—salvation through Jesus. What a blessing to see some of them turn to Christ as a result! You don't have to be a preacher to help people with their problems. Many lost people seek advice from Christian friends and coworkers. That is why you need to *"be ready always to give an answer to every man that asketh you a reason of the hope that is in you with meekness and fear"* (1 Peter 3:15).

Try using the "by-the-way" method to change the subject to spiritual matters when there is a lull in the conversation. It is abrupt but not awkward. People change subjects all the time when conversing with one another. Simply say, "By the way, I've been thinking a lot lately about what happens after death and was wondering if you have given it much thought. Do you know for sure that you will go to Heaven when you die?" You might be surprised that they have been thinking about it too. Even if they haven't, you might have piqued their interest. In either case, this may give you a green light to share what you have learned from the Bible.

Ask God to help you to know what to say, and He will guide you. When Moses lacked confidence to speak on

Simple Soulwinning Steps

God's behalf, the Lord gave him a wonderful promise—*"I will be with thy mouth"* (Exodus 4:12). Certainly, God can assist you too! There are few things more exciting than experiencing God supernaturally working through you to help bring someone to Christ.

Witnessing to Family and Friends

For some reason, witnessing to friends and relatives can be a bit intimidating. We shouldn't be scared because we know and love them, and they care for us too. Despite our mutual affection for each other, it can still be difficult. Perhaps we are afraid they won't want to discuss spiritual matters, or maybe we think they will be offended. Regardless of what causes us to fear, we need to be bold and show our concern. You might start out by saying, "I've wanted to talk to you about something very important." That sets the stage. Since they care about you, whatever is important to you must be worth discussing.

The Bible records many examples of people bringing their loved ones to Jesus. Andrew *"first findeth his own brother Simon"* (John 1:41). The converted maniac went to his home and told them about the *"great things"* Christ had done for him (Luke 8:39). In desperation, the Syrophenician woman brought her daughter who was *"grievously vexed with a devil"* to Jesus for healing (Matthew 15:21-28). Four men carried their friend to

Jesus on a bed and helped him find forgiveness (Mark 2:1-5). These accounts show one common thread—we should not delay witnessing to our family and friends.

As we have already seen, God commands us to go and preach the gospel. Since it is not always easy to witness, we are tempted to find ways to get out of doing it. Let's address that matter next.

Don't Make Excuses

Since winning souls is a spiritual matter, you can rest assured that the flesh wants little to do with it. Sometimes we get all fired up about witnessing and then find our fervency begins to wane. We intend to witness more but not right away. If you find yourself making excuses for not witnessing, you are not alone. Jesus told us what often hinders our good intentions. He said, *"...the spirit indeed is willing, but the flesh is weak"* (Matthew 26:41). Whether we like to admit it or not, we are weak, but thankfully, God's Word strengthens us to overcome our natural frailties. So, let's examine some common excuses that we make for not witnessing and consider them in light of the Bible.

First, "I am afraid." Fear probably hinders Christians more than anything else when it comes to witnessing. We are afraid of being rejected, reviled, and ridiculed. We fear people that might intimidate us such as hardened sinners, highly educated intellectuals, or

Simple Soulwinning Steps

religious scholars. Fear has kept multitudes of lost people from hearing a gospel witness or receiving a tract. The truth is that most people have fear. That is why God put commands such as *"fear not"* and *"be not afraid"* in the Bible dozens of times. When Joshua was given an overwhelming task, he did not feel adequate. Notice what God told him—*"Have not I commanded thee? Be strong and of a good courage; be not afraid, neither be thou dismayed: for the LORD thy God is with thee whithersoever thou goest"* (Joshua 1:9).

It is up to us as individuals to exercise faith instead of fear. Consider what Jesus said to the disciples, *"And he said unto them, Why are ye so fearful? how is it that ye have no faith?"* (Mark 4:40). They were fearful because they had no faith. Fear is a decision, not merely an emotion. We can do something about our fear. We can choose faith instead of fear. So, saying, "I'm afraid" is not a legitimate excuse.

Second, "I am too busy." We all have the same number of hours in a day, and we choose how we will use them. If Jesus' purpose for coming to earth was to seek and save lost people, shouldn't that be a priority in our lives too? The apostle Paul encourages us to proclaim the gospel when it is convenient and when it does not fit into our schedule. He said, *"Preach the word; be instant in season, out of season"* (2 Timothy 4:2). We should have a *"season"* to witness such as a scheduled time to go soulwinning. However, we are

Follow God's Plan

also responsible to witness *"out of season."* As you can see, being too busy to witness is disobedience. It is certainly not an acceptable excuse.

Third, *"I would, but I don't know what to say."* This almost sounds like a legitimate excuse. It is usually used by those who do not have much experience in witnessing. The truth is that even a brand new Christian can witness for the Lord. Consider the example of the maniac of Gadara. Immediately after he was saved, Jesus told him to witness to others—*"And when he was come into the ship, he that had been possessed with the devil prayed him that he might be with him. Howbeit Jesus suffered him not, but saith unto him, Go home to thy friends, and tell them how great things the Lord hath done for thee, and hath had compassion on thee"* (Mark 5:18-19). This man did not know much about the Bible, but he knew what God had done for him. Jesus had changed his life! So, he *"began to publish…how great things Jesus had done for him: and all men did marvel"* (Mark 5:20). Despite being a new believer, his efforts were impressive!

If you don't know what to say, start by telling people what Jesus did for you. Then, begin to study the Bible so that you can become even more effective. Since the formerly demon-possessed man started witnessing right after he was saved, we have no excuse not to do the same.

Simple Soulwinning Steps

Fourth, "I don't have the gift of evangelism." Neither does anybody else because there is no such gift. When you look at the gifts given to Christians in Romans 12, evangelism is not listed. Paul told Timothy to *"do the work of an evangelist"* (2 Timothy 4:5). Did you notice the word *work*? The truth is that evangelizing the lost is hard work. Though none of us has a gift to witness, we all have a command to do it. Jesus said, *"Go ye into all the world, and preach the gospel to every creature"* (Mark 16:15). Let's stop making excuses and get busy.

Fifth, "I thought soulwinning was the pastor's job!" This is what we call "passing the buck." The Great Commission was given to the local church, not just the pastor. Jesus said, *"Herein is my Father glorified, that ye bear much fruit; so shall ye be my disciples"* (John 15:8). Winning souls is the job of every disciple, not only a task for preachers. It is true that a good pastor will be involved in witnessing to others, but he does so because that is what all good Christians do. As a pastor, his duty is *"the perfecting of the saints"* so that they can do *"the work of the ministry"* (Ephesians 4:12). We ought to rejoice if we have a pastor who not only wins souls, but also equips and challenges us to do likewise!

Sixth, "People are not interested these days so it is no use." Really? The disciples of Jesus made a similar excuse, and Jesus scolded them for it. He said, *"Say not ye, There are yet four months, and then cometh harvest?*

behold, I say unto you, Lift up your eyes, and look on the fields; for they are white already to harvest" (John 4:35). The disciples basically said, "We don't have to worry about the harvest right now because the crop is not ripe." If you take the time to study John 4, you will see that the disciples had just returned from the city of Samaria. They apparently made no effort to evangelize while visiting the city because they thought the people were not ripe for the picking. Meanwhile, the woman that Jesus had met at the well got saved while the disciples were in the city. She eagerly returned to the same city and had great success in witnessing. It is amazing that seasoned disciples were less effective than a new convert! How could this be? The disciples fell into the trap that many of us fall into—they thought people were not interested in the gospel.

It can be discouraging to witness at times, especially when the results seem few. Not everyone is interested, but there are some who are ready to be saved. We will not find them if we remain silent and assume that nobody will respond to the gospel. Jesus said that *"the fields...are white already to harvest."* Is He a liar? No!

When I travel, I typically give a tract to the hotel employee who checks me in. Some are cordial but not eager to discuss the gospel, but others are friendly and appreciative. I recall giving a tract to a young lady one evening, and she got choked up and responded, "I really need this right now." I took that as an open door to

Simple Soulwinning Steps

share the gospel. As a result, she made a decision to trust Christ as her Savior! It has been my experience that even though not everyone I witness to is interested, some people are. Whether someone seems interested or not, we should still try to witness. That's the only way we will find out who is.

Consider the maniac of Gadara again. Before his conversion, he certainly did not seem like someone desiring to be with Jesus. He ran around naked, lived in tombs, cut himself, was not in his right mind, and terrorized his community. He would probably have been voted least likely to be interested in salvation in his hometown. However, of all the people who came into contact with Jesus that day, he was the only one to be saved. Looks can be deceiving. We can't tell what is going on in a person's heart. The conversion of the maniac teaches us that the most hardened people can be the ones closest to salvation.

Years ago while flying to Denver, I was seated beside an 18-year-old man who looked like a hippie. The Lord urged me to witness to him, but I made the age-old excuse, "He's probably not interested in the Bible." I shrugged off God's leading throughout the flight. As we approached the airport, the pilot announced that our plane had to be diverted to another airport, extending our flight by about forty minutes. I remember thinking, "Okay, Lord. You win. I'll witness to him." Contrary to what I thought, the young man was quite receptive to

Follow God's Plan

the gospel. Just before the plane landed, he bowed his head and received Christ as his Savior. Remember that the devil is a liar, and he rejoices when we judge people unworthy of our witness. Satan wants us to believe that nobody is interested. Jesus said that *"the fields...are white already to harvest"* (John 4:35). Who will you believe?

As you can see, we really have no excuses. God wants us to witness to the lost, and we must be about our Father's business. It is one thing to know what we are supposed to do and another thing to do it. So, let's get busy and stop making excuses!

LESSON FOUR

Fill Your Heart and Head

All Christians should continually develop their lives to become more useful for the Lord. Jude reminded his fellow believers, *"But ye, beloved, building up yourselves on your most holy faith"* (Jude 20). We are expected to study God's Word and build upon what we already know. One way to polish up on our knowledge of the Scriptures is to memorize verses that can be used in our soulwinning efforts.

The Bible is called *"the sword of the Spirit"* (Ephesians 6:7). It is what God uses to prick hearts and produce conviction in the lost. The writer of Hebrews said, *"For the word of God is quick, and powerful, and sharper than any twoedged sword, piercing even to the dividing asunder of soul and spirit, and of the joints and marrow, and is a discerner of the thoughts and intents of the heart"* (Hebrews 4:12). Since God uses His Word, it would be a shame if we did not know it well enough to share with others! God's Word is a powerful Sword, and it is our duty to wield it as skillful swordsmen. The better we know the Bible, the more effectively we can evangelize the lost.

Simple Soulwinning Steps

As a soulwinner, it is a good start to know where to find important verses in the Bible. However, we become even more capable witnesses when we commit key verses to memory. Therefore, we should fill our hearts and heads with Scripture. Let's see why it is important to memorize the Bible, and then we will consider some tips to make memorization easier.

Importance of Memorizing Verses

Many people become overwhelmed with the thought of memorizing Bible verses. Some think it's almost impossible, while others cringe when they consider the effort involved. It is amazing how we can memorize phone numbers, words to songs, addresses, etc., but we dread doing the same with the Bible. If you can remember other things, the Lord will certainly help you recall His Word! In fact, He has promised to help us. *"But the Comforter, which is the Holy Ghost, whom the Father will send in my name, he shall teach you all things, and bring all things to your remembrance, whatsoever I have said unto you"* (John 14:26). You see, if you put it in your heart, the Holy Spirit will help you remember it when it is needed!

You may ask, "Why do I have to memorize verses? Can't I just remember where to look them up?" Here's why you should memorize Scripture:

Fill Your Heart and Head

1. God wants us to do it! Consider what God says about hiding His Word in our hearts.

   "The law of his God is in his heart; none of his steps shall slide" (Psalm 37:31).

   "Thy word have I hid in mine heart, that I might not sin against thee" (Psalm 119:11).

   "For it is a pleasant thing if thou keep them within thee; they shall withal be fitted in thy lips" (Proverbs 22:18).

   "But sanctify the Lord God in your hearts: and be ready always to give an answer to every man that asketh you a reason of the hope that is in you with meekness and fear" (1 Peter 3:15).

2. It allows you to witness to others when you do not have a Bible with you.

3. It helps you remember where to find verses in the Bible.

4. It enables the Holy Spirit to lead you to the right Scriptures to use at the right time. Because everybody has different needs, the Lord will guide you to use different verses.

5. You earn the respect of your hearers when they see that you know what you are talking about.

Simple Soulwinning Steps

Tips for Memorizing and Remembering

People use a variety of methods to memorize, and you need to find what works best for you. However, educators tell us that learning is more effective when you engage more of your senses. The five senses are seeing, hearing, smelling, touching, and tasting. Using two or more senses will help you to learn better than only using one. In the following points, we will consider five learning tools that are similar to the five senses. Let us briefly consider:

1. **Seeing** – Read each verse aloud five times every morning and five times in the evening before going to bed. Do this for seven days.

2. **Hearing** – If you read the verses aloud, you are also hearing them at the same time! This helps you to learn them better than if you only read them silently.

3. **Speaking** – Another benefit of reading the verses aloud is that a third method, speaking, is used! Got it yet? Read aloud!

4. **Writing** – Writing uses the sense of touch and is a great learning tool. The more you write something down, the easier it becomes to remember it. I suggest that you write verses on index cards to carry in your pocket for studying

Fill Your Heart and Head

throughout the week. Writing them in a notebook by subject can also help.

5. **Tasting** – How do you taste a verse? You can do it figuratively. The psalmist said, *"O taste and see that the LORD is good"* (Psalm 34:8). By trying to use the verse in daily conversation, you taste it by seeing how good it is in real-life situations. We all know that experience can be a great teacher!

Don't forget to review your verses every week. For instance, after learning the first set of memory verses, look them over once a day for next several weeks as you continue learning new verses. So, while learning the second set of verses, review the ones from the first set daily. Continue reviewing each lesson's verses for at least four weeks, and you will be surprised how they will stick in your mind!

If you are struggling with learning a long verse, simply break the verse up into phrases. Learn the verse phrase by phrase until you can put it all together. There are also apps available for your cellphone that help with verse memory work. Here's one last bit of advice for memorizing. Be sure to memorize the subject and Scripture reference along with each verse. Consider the following example:

Simple Soulwinning Steps

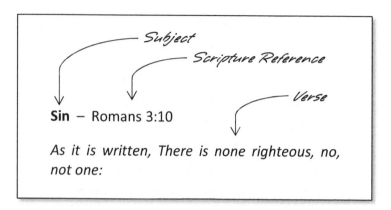

Hopefully, you are excited about learning God's Word so that you can share it with others. Future lessons in this book will include memory challenges to help you become a more effective witness. With the above tips about memorizing Scripture, you should feel more equipped to do so than ever before!

LESSON FIVE

Be Flexible

Although it is good to have a general plan to follow when presenting the gospel, we must remember that no two people are exactly alike. Each person has different needs. That means every soulwinning presentation will vary. It is our duty to perceive the needs of the people and adjust our message as the Holy Spirit guides us. In other words, we must be flexible when witnessing. Here are a few tips you can follow.

Determine Your Direction

There are basically two types of lost people in this world: religious sinners and non-religious sinners. It is important to know the spiritual background of people when witnessing so that you know the right direction to take. You can do this by asking people if they currently attend church or if they attended while growing up.

Dealing with Religious Sinners – When people claim to be religious, they typically follow the teachings of their church regarding salvation. By knowing what church they attend, you can get an idea of what they have been taught. Most denominations teach a works-based salvation, stressing the need to follow specific

Simple Soulwinning Steps

church teachings in order to be forgiven. Once you know their church background, you will have a better idea of what Scriptures to use with them. For example, if someone is a Roman Catholic, he believes that baptism washes away original sin. Showing great compassion, you can share verses that show otherwise. One of the main goals you should have while dealing with religious people is to help them to see that their good works do not save them. This is addressed in greater detail later in this book.

Dealing with Non-Religious Sinners – In America, things have changed. The majority of people in our society used to be churchgoers. Now there are more people who openly state that they are not religious. Since they lack basic, foundational knowledge about God, they require a different approach. Rather than assuming that they believe basic doctrines accepted by most denominations, such as the deity of Christ or the existence of hell, they will need an overview of the Bible. This of course begins with Who God is and what He is like. Even though the average person today thinks creation is a myth, they must understand that God is their Creator. Rather than delve into a long debate about evolution vs. creation, it is better to try to present creation as fact. Then proceed to explain that because God is the Creator, He has the right to make the rules for His creation. By explaining the fall of man, you can show how sin entered the world. Then, make it

Be Flexible

personal and go through some of the Ten Commandments, showing that we all have sinned. This leads naturally to discussing judgment for sin. Most people understand that criminals should be judged for their actions, which allows you to show how God will judge those who break His laws. Then, you can tell them that there is good news—God sent His Son Jesus to take the punishment that we deserve. You can say, "Perhaps you have heard of the Trinity. God is actually three people in One—the Father, the Son Jesus, and the Holy Spirit." Tell them how Jesus left Heaven to become a sinless substitute for our sin, and explain that what He did on the cross provides a way for us to be forgiven. Encourage them to repent and trust Jesus Christ to forgive them and change their lives. Without Jesus they have *"no hope"* (Ephesians 2:12). You offer a message they truly need!

In later lessons, we will discuss verses that can be used to teach the great truths we mentioned above. The content of a gospel tract that I wrote entitled, *What's the Bible All About?*, is included in Appendix B. It may provide some helpful ideas that you can incorporate when witnessing to someone who lacks a foundation of Biblical knowledge.

Simple Soulwinning Steps

Adjust Your Presentation

It is good to have an idea of how you will begin your witness, but, as you are probably beginning to see, you will have to make adjustments along the way. Consider two ways in which you may need to alter your presentation.

Adjust What You Say – As you learn more about what a person believes, focus on what he needs to hear most. For example, if you are witnessing to a Jehovah's Witness, you would stress the deity of Christ rather than warn against trusting the sacraments for salvation as you would a Roman Catholic. When someone finds it difficult to believe that they do not have to do good works to be saved, you will have to use more Scripture to prove it.

Adjust How Much You Say – It is important to gauge how much time you have to present the gospel. If someone tells you that he has to leave for work in thirty minutes, don't be overzealous and try to witness to him for an hour! Learn to wrap things up the best you can with the time that you have. Always try to leave the door open to return at a more convenient time. In some cases, you know that your paths will not cross again. When that happens, try to finish by giving a quick summary of the gospel, leave a good tract, and encourage the person to make a decision to receive Jesus as soon as possible.

Be Flexible

Personalize Your Presentation

It is important to try to identify with the person to whom you are witnessing. Be concerned for people, not critical of them and their beliefs. If you come across in a condescending manner, you will quickly lose your audience. However, if you demonstrate that you are human, having the same questions and fears, you can endear your listener to your message. There are two helpful ways to personalize your gospel presentation: share your testimony and acknowledge their comments.

Share Your Testimony – Every Christian has a unique testimony. Part of witnessing is telling people what God has done in your life. As a soulwinner, always look for common ground with your listeners. By expressing what God has shown you, they will learn how God can help them. Thankfully, God not only expects us to witness for Him but also enables us to do so. Jesus said, *"But ye shall receive power, after that the Holy Ghost is come upon you: and ye shall be witnesses unto me"* (Acts 1:8). Your testimony does not have to be long or complicated. Here are a few things you may want to include: what your life was like before you were saved, what you believed prior to salvation, how you heard the gospel, your initial reaction to the gospel, and the changes that God has made since you were saved. Your testimony provides a human element to a heavenly message. It tells of a real-life experience with a real God, and that brings hope to lost sinners.

Acknowledge Their Comments – Learn to ask what people think and incorporate their input into the conversation. There will usually be things that you agree on, and by recognizing their thoughts, you will earn their respect and keep their attention. For example, when talking about sin, the sinner may say that nobody is perfect. You can say, "You're right. That's exactly what the Bible says." Then you can proceed to share Romans 3:23, *"For all have sinned, and come short of the glory of God."* Including their statements shows that you are willing to listen, not just lecture. You must remember that you are having a conversation. You are not preaching a sermon in which your hearers are expected to remain silent. If we fail to engage our listeners in dialogue, we will not know what they are thinking, and that makes it difficult to know how to proceed with the gospel presentation. So, be personable and come across more as a concerned friend than a caustic interrogator or pompous tutor.

Observe Reactions

It is the soulwinner's job to read people. Don't develop tunnel vision by focusing more on *what* you say than on *how* your message is received. If someone is not paying attention to what you say, they are not going

Be Flexible

to get saved. So, look for the following: interest, understanding, conviction, and repentance.

Interest – It is good to realize when people have no interest in the gospel. When you think they might be indifferent, try to verify your hunch by making an effort to capture their attention. One of the best ways to do this is to ask questions to get them involved. For instance, you can ask, "So, what do you think will happen to you if you die without having your sins forgiven?" Once you hear their response, you not only have their attention but also know how to proceed with the conversation.

Understanding – Doctrinal terminology and Biblical vocabulary can seem like foreign words to many people. The natural man has limited comprehension of spiritual matters. Paul explained this well, *"But the natural man receiveth not the things of the Spirit of God: for they are foolishness unto him: neither can he know them, because they are spiritually discerned"* (1 Corinthians 2:14). When Philip saw the Ethiopian man reading the Scriptures he said, *"Understandest thou what thou readest?"* (Acts 8:30). How did the man respond? He replied, *"How can I, except some man should guide me?"* (Acts 8:31). The job of the soulwinner is to help sinners understand God's Word. Look for comprehension. Then, be ready to explain and illustrate your message.

Conviction –The Holy Spirit produces conviction in the hearts of people. Jesus said of the Spirit, *"And when*

Simple Soulwinning Steps

he is come, he will reprove the world of sin, and of righteousness, and of judgment" (John 16:8). As we saw earlier, the word *reprove* means "to convict; to convince." Though we cannot see what is going on in the heart of an individual, we can often observe conviction by words that are spoken or by facial expressions. If someone is convinced of the truth, it will be apparent. Just remember that not everyone responds to conviction in the same way. Sometimes people are eager to hear more and will say something like, *"...what must I do to be saved?"* (Acts 16:30). Other times people might get angry and hostile. That is what happened when Philip witnessed to the council—*"When they heard these things, they were cut to the heart, and they gnashed on him with their teeth"* (Acts 7:54). Just remember that some people are more expressive than others. Just because a person does not show a lot of outward emotion does not mean they are not under conviction. If they are convinced about the point you are making from the Scripture, you can proceed to your next point. If they are not, you should share more of God's Word until they are convinced.

Repentance – The word *repent* refers to a change of mind. When witnessing, we should ultimately look for a change of mind about sin. People must realize that their sin separates them from God and His blessings. Also, they need to change their minds about what they trust for salvation. For instance, if a Catholic man still thinks that baptism washes away sin after you have presented the gospel to him, he has not repented. He is not ready to be saved. As soulwinners, we should not lead someone to receive Christ as Savior if they have not lined up their thinking with the Word of God.

Follow the Holy Spirit's Guidance

Although you do not know the spiritual needs of each person you talk to, God does. As a soulwinner, you must allow the Holy Spirit to guide you to use the specific verses that each individual needs to hear. Throughout your presentation of the gospel, maintain a spirit of prayer and look to the Lord for guidance. He will *"...guide you into all truth"* (John 16:13). As you depend on the Lord, you will be amazed how He can work through you in a supernatural way! Don't be overwhelmed with how difficult it might be to witness to someone. Instead, be overjoyed with how much God has promised to help you to spread the good news. Notice the presence of God experienced by the disciples when they witnessed—*"And they went forth, and preached every where, the Lord working with them"* (Mark 16:20). The Lord wants to work with you too!

Conclusion

In the next few lessons, we will discuss some of the basic points to include when presenting the gospel.

Simple Soulwinning Steps

Since every person has specific needs, consider the following lessons as a guide. You will not use every verse mentioned in each lesson when you witness, and you might be led to use verses that are not even discussed in this book. Hopefully, you will glean something from each lesson that will enable you to lead sinners to the Savior.

At the conclusion of the following chapters, you will be challenged to memorize key Bible verses. By committing God's Word to memory, you will be better equipped to point people to Jesus.

LESSON SIX

Anticipate Objections

Not every sinner will welcome your message with open arms. Some people may come across as skeptical or antagonistic. However, you must not be thrown off by negative reactions. In many cases, things are not always as they seem.

My father has been a soulwinner for over fifty years. He takes an optimistic approach when dealing with objections. He says, "An objection is nothing more than an unanswered question or a request for more information." In other words, many people who raise objections are really hoping that you have an answer for something that has puzzled them for a while. Instead of getting offended or uptight when people express their ignorance about spiritual matters, we should see it as an opportunity to help them understand the truth.

Some objections are more crucial to answer than others. For instance, if someone says that people are good and there is no such thing as sin, you have to address that before continuing with the plan of salvation. Thankfully, the Bible clearly defines sin. However, some objections are ridiculous. For instance, some people like to get you flustered by saying

Simple Soulwinning Steps

something foolish like, "Can God make a rock so big that He can't pick it up?" In this case, *"Answer a fool according to his folly"* (Proverbs 26:5). Tell him that God is Almighty and not to be trifled with. People who ask silly questions like this are typically just trying to be a "wise guy." Don't let their antics phase you. Get back to the gospel and pray that they begin to fear God when the Scriptures are read to them.

Here are a few common objections and some brief suggestions on how to handle them:

"I don't believe in God."

Obviously, people who say that they do not believe in God lack faith. How does someone gain faith? *"So then faith cometh by hearing, and hearing by the word of God"* (Romans 10:17). The best thing you can do is give them Scripture. I recall witnessing to a man on the streets of Chicago. He told me that he was an atheist. However, he was willing to listen to the Bible. At the end of our conversation, though he did not get saved, he was one step closer because he realized that God exists. There is power in the Word of God! Such a change of mind does not happen with everyone who claims to be an atheist. I remember another self-professed atheist that I witnessed to in a middle-class neighborhood. We talked for well over an hour. For every objection he gave, the Lord gave me a verse to answer him. He slowly became frustrated because his arguments had fallen apart. I told him that I did not believe he was really an atheist because if he was, he wouldn't have wasted so much time talking about Someone Who supposedly didn't exist. I discovered that the man had a relative who had been witnessing to him. It appeared to me that his objections were really a plea for me to prove that God really existed. When you find yourself in situations like this, remember that one sows, another waters, and God gives the increase. Be content to do your part.

Perhaps the best approach to take with an atheist is to give your testimony. Share how God changed your life. It is difficult for people to refute the evident hand of God in someone's life. If the person is willing, ask if you can share a few Scriptures that changed your life. This just might be what they need most!

"If God is so good, why does He let bad things happen to people?"

Behind this question is often a hurting heart. While canvassing one day, I recall meeting a man who had grown bitter toward God. He was a middle-aged fellow who had challenging health problems. In addition to his many ailments, he had recently been told that he was going blind. He further relayed how his brother had been in a wheelchair for most of his life and had to be cared for by his aging father. Unfortunately, like many people, this man turned against God instead of turning to Him. When dealing with people like this, you will not fix their problems in one visit. Show empathy, but insist that God is not to be blamed for the world's problems or injustices. Remind them that sin ruined God's perfect creation. Sickness and death originated from man's disobedience to God. Tragedies such as rape, murder, and violent crimes stem from the hearts of sinners. Remind people that Jesus came to save us from sin and bring us to a much better place—Heaven. Try to lovingly explain that Christ came to *"heal the brokenhearted"* (Luke 4:18).

"How can a loving God send people to hell?"

Once again, we see man's attempt to find fault with God. To answer this objection, start by confirming that there is a hell and explain that people go there because of sin. Then share with them that God loved us so much that He provided a way for us to be forgiven of our sin. Explain that God has more than one characteristic. He is holy. Therefore, He hates sin. He is just. So, He must punish sin. God is love. That is why He sent His Son to be punished in our place. You can quote John 3:16, Isaiah 53:6, and 2 Corinthians 5:21. Try to get people to see that God is not at fault; they are. The Lord has done everything possible to prevent people from going to

Anticipate Objections

hell. If someone goes there, it is because they rejected God's way of salvation (Revelation 21:8).

"I'm not so bad. I'm a pretty good person."

The person might be good compared to other people in society but not compared to God's standards. Remind them that our opinion of ourselves is not as important as what God says about us. Take them to Romans 3:10—*"As it is written, There is none righteous, no, not one."* Emphasize the words *"not one."* Then read 1 John 1:8—*"If we say that we have no sin, we deceive ourselves, and the truth is not in us."* If the person still struggles to admit that he is a sinner, read one of the many passages that lists common sins (Romans 1:29-32, 1 Corinthians 6:9-10, and Galatians 5:19-21). Though this objection is easy to answer, it does not mean that the sinner will like the answer.

"God is merciful. So, I should be fine."

This objection might be offered by a sincere person who knows a little about the Bible but not enough. While it is true that God is merciful, He has requirements to receive His mercy. In Ephesians 2:4, we see that God *"is rich in mercy."* However, a few verses later Paul explained that salvation comes through faith—*"For by grace are ye saved through faith; and that not of yourselves: it is the gift of God"* (Ephesians 2:8). It is one thing to acknowledge that God is merciful and quite another thing to depend solely upon Christ for forgiveness. Receiving mercy also requires repentance. When David cried for mercy, he was broken over his sin and confessed his transgressions (Psalm 51:1-4). Therefore, no sinner can presume upon the mercy of God to overlook their sin. Every sinner must acknowledge his sinfulness, repent of his sin, and place his faith in Christ to cleanse and regenerate him. See also Titus 3:5.

"The Bible is full of contradictions."

Simply say, "Show me one." That usually ends that argument because there are no errors in the Word of God. Even if someone can point to an apparent contradiction, by comparing Scripture with Scripture, you can clarify their misunderstandings. Here are a couple of good verses to use for this objection—*"The words of the LORD are pure words"* (Psalm 12:6) and *"Every word of God is pure: he is a shield unto them that put their trust in him"* (Proverbs 30:5). The Bible is perfect because it came from God—*"For the prophecy came not in old time by the will of man: but holy men of God spake as they were moved by the Holy Ghost"* (2 Peter 1:21). Once again, share a testimony of how God has used His Word in your life. Tell how its principles have guided you and how its promises have blessed you. Never forget how powerful your testimony is.

"All roads lead to Heaven."

Do all roads lead to New York? No. Do all roads lead to Los Angeles? Certainly not. Even common sense disproves this argument. This is usually spoken by someone who does not want to believe that Jesus is the only way to Heaven. To refute this objection, take the person straight to John 14:6—*"Jesus saith unto him, I am the way, the truth, and the life: no man cometh unto the Father, but by me."* The Scripture is clear that Christ is the only way! Consider also Acts 4:12, *"Neither is there salvation in any other: for there is none other name under heaven given among men, whereby we must be saved."* Paul also was emphatic that Jesus was the only way to God—*"For there is one God, and one mediator between God and men, the man Christ Jesus"* (1 Timothy 2:5).

"I know someone who goes to church, and he is a hypocrite."

A simple way to answer this is to explain that Jesus is against hypocrites too. In fact some of His harshest words were reserved for religious hypocrites (Matthew 23:13-33). Tell the person complaining about hypocrites that they are just the kind of person Jesus is looking for! Tell them that if they get saved, they can help set a good example in the church. It should not be shocking that hypocrites are found in churches. After all, the Bible says, *"For all have sinned, and come short of the glory of God"* (Romans 3:23). Everyone in the world is a sinner and will struggle to be genuine at times. If the person giving this objection is honest, he will admit that not every churchgoer that he knows is a hypocrite. Explain it this way, "Sir, there are a lot of bad people in the world. Some bad people shop at Walmart, but we don't judge the store by a few customers. Some bad people attend the town's schools, but an entire school system shouldn't be condemned because of a few bad students. Does one bad person in your neighborhood make all of the neighbors bad? No." Hopefully, you can tactfully answer this objection and bring the conversation back to his need for the Lord. Too many people just want to point fingers at others in an attempt to escape personal responsibility.

Conclusion

There are too many possible objections to list here. Paul described a good approach to take when handling objections—*"And the servant of the Lord must not strive; but be gentle unto all men, apt to teach, patient, In meekness instructing those that oppose themselves; if God peradventure will give them repentance to the acknowledging of the truth"* (2 Timothy 2:24-25). Resist the temptation to *"strive"* and get into an argument. Be

Anticipate Objections

patient with people and try to provide them with an answer from Scripture. Don't let a question or comment stump you. Silently pray for wisdom, and you will be amazed at how the Lord helps in such situations. Do your best to resolve their objection and get back to the plan of salvation.

Part Two

What to Say

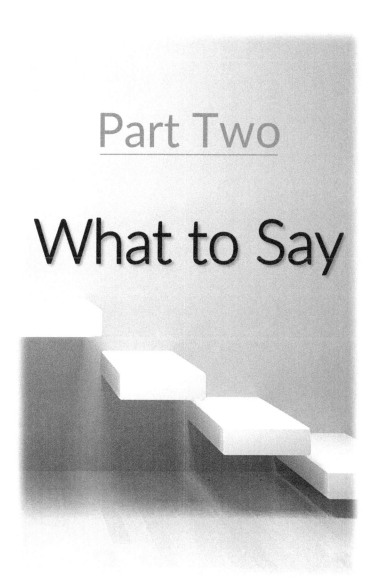

LESSON SEVEN

God Loves Us, Not Our Sin

Finally, we get to the nitty-gritty of soulwinning. In the lessons that follow, we will discuss the main topics that should be included in a presentation of the gospel. We begin first with the matter of sin.

The purpose of this lesson is to show a person that he is a sinner and needs to be saved. This can be a sensitive issue for some people, and you do not want to be rude in your approach. God tells us how we should handle this situation, *"And of some have compassion, making a difference..."* (Jude 22). So, instead of accusing them of noticeable sins in their lives, gently guide them through the Scripture to see that all people, including you, are guilty of sin.

We have to figure out how to get onto the subject of sin. If you start the conversation by saying, "You are a sinner on your way to hell," you will probably lose your audience quite quickly. However, if we *"have compassion"* and show some empathy, it can make a big difference. I suggest starting with God's love. Show people John 3:16 and explain that God loves them and

Simple Soulwinning Steps

sent His Son to die for them. From there, you can ask them if they know why Jesus had to die. This allows you to explain that, although God loves all people, He does not love their sin. Then, you can tell them how sin separates us from God's blessings and ultimately keeps us out of Heaven.

By getting people to see sin as their foe, they will see that you are on their side, not against them. After all, most of us don't like to be told that we are wrong, especially by total strangers! So, help the lost to see what they are missing out on because of their sin. Certainly, sin keeps us out of Heaven, but it has many other negative consequences. Explain that God loves them very much and has a wonderful plan for their lives. You can even testify how God answers prayer, gives peace, and provides for His children. Then tell them that we miss out on those things because of sin. Jeremiah 5:25 is a great verse to use at this point, *"Your iniquities have turned away these things, and your sins have withholden good things from you."* This approach can be a helpful transition to discussing sin.

Another way to get the conversation started is to ask the person if they have ever heard of the term *saved* and what they think it might mean. Explain that being saved refers to being delivered. That naturally leads to the next question—delivered from what? You can share how Jesus came to save us from sin and its consequences (Matthew 1:21).

God Loves Us, Not Our Sin

Here is an example of how you can guide people to acknowledge their sin:

You: "Some people wonder what life is all about. Thankfully, we don't have to wonder. The Bible shows us that God loves us and has a wonderful plan for our lives."

Read: *"For God so loved the world, that he gave his only begotten Son, that whosoever believeth in him should not perish, but have everlasting life"* (John 3:16).

You: "Do you know why God sent His Son to earth?"

Friend: "To die for us?"

You: "Yes, He came to die for our sin. Although God loves us, He hates our sin. Allow me to use an example. Parents typically love their children, but they don't reward bad behavior with blessings. In the same way, our sin hinders us from receiving many of God's blessings."

You: "Perhaps you have heard of the word *saved* before. Have you ever wondered what it means? It means to be rescued or delivered. What do you think we need to be saved or rescued from?"

Simple Soulwinning Steps

Friend: "Ourselves, I guess."

You: "That's part of it. We need to be saved from our sin. God wants everyone to go to Heaven, but there is something that will keep us out—sin. Allow me to illustrate this. Let's pretend you were a child again and your mother had just bought a new white carpet. Would she allow you to come into the house wearing muddy shoes?"

Friend: "There's no way! Not my mom."

You: "Most moms wouldn't! You would have to take your shoes off first and get cleaned up to go in. Likewise, God's Heaven is clean, and sin is dirty. God cannot allow you into Heaven with sin. You must have your sins washed away."

You: "Pretending that we do not have sin won't solve our problem. So let's see what God has to say about sin."

Now, you need to begin to use Scripture to show people that they are guilty of sin. The chart below provides verses that you can use to convince them of their sinful condition. Simply read a verse and explain it. You do not have to read all of the verses, but you should

God Loves Us, Not Our Sin

use enough Scripture to make sure they understand that **they** are sinners. Occasionally, you may meet people who deny that they are sinners. There are verses listed below for that too. People must acknowledge their guilt before they can be saved.

Verses Showing the Fact of Sin	Verses for Those Who Do Not Admit Being a Sinner
1. Romans 3:10	1. 1 John 1:8, 10
2. Romans 3:23	2. Revelation 21:8
3. Isaiah 53:6	3. Romans 1:29-32
4. Isaiah 64:6	4. Galatians 5:19-21

Here is what you can say as you discuss the fact of sin:

Read: *"As it is written, There is none righteous, no, not one"* (Romans 3:10).

You: "According to this verse, are you righteous?"

Friend: "No, none of us are."

You: "That word *righteous* means good enough to go to Heaven."

Read: *"For all have sinned, and come short of the glory of God"* (Romans 3:23).

You: "How many of us have sinned?"

Simple Soulwinning Steps

Friend: "All of us. None of us are perfect."

You: "Right. That includes me and you. What are some common sins that people commit?"

Friend: "Stealing, lying, murder..."

You: "Right. There's a lot of them: adultery, taking God's name in vain, cursing, covetousness, etc."

Read: *"Now we know that what things soever the law saith, it saith to them who are under the law: that every mouth may be stopped, and all the world may become guilty before God."* (Romans 3:19).

You: "The Bible says that we are all guilty of breaking God's Law. The Law refers to the Ten Commandments."

Read: Turn to Exodus 20:3-17 and discuss a few of the Ten Commandments: obey parents, don't lie, don't steal, don't take God's name in vain, don't commit adultery, etc.

You: "Have you broken any of God's Commandments?"

Friend: "We all have."

You: "That's right. We are all guilty of sin. Next,

God Loves Us, Not Our Sin

we will see what God thinks about our sin and what will happen to those who do not accept God's way of forgiveness."

Simple Soulwinning Steps

Memory Challenge for Lesson 7

Memorize and recite the following verses:

Sin – Romans 3:10
As it is written, There is none righteous, no, not one:

_____   _____
Instructor's Signature   Date

Sin – Romans 3:23
For all have sinned, and come short of the glory of God;

_____   _____
Instructor's Signature   Date

Additional Verses:

Verses	Instructor's Signature	Date
Isaiah 53:6		
Isaiah 64:6		
1 John 1:8		
1 John 1:10		

LESSON EIGHT

Sin Has to Be Punished

In previous generations, people were raised with the idea that wrongdoing should be punished. Today, however, our society struggles just to know the difference between right and wrong. Politicians, schools, and the media promote tolerance of behavior that deviates from the Bible. With no moral compass, it is not only difficult to identify evil but also to condemn it. As a result, sin often goes unchecked.

The idea of punishment seems to be growing more unacceptable with each passing day. For instance, parents are taught that if they love their children, they should not chasten them. Therefore, children are raised with little discipline and often do as they please without much correction. When they become adults, they think that if God loves them, He would not possibly punish them in a fiery hell. To make matters worse, an increasing number of preachers are teaching the same thing.

How deceived people have become! So, what is the solution to this problem? Simply show them what God says. Trust the power of the Word of God to convince unbelieving hearts. It has effectively worked through the ages and is no less capable today.

Faithfully present the truths of the Bible and, in a concerned manner, show people that punishment and suffering will result from sin. Thankfully, most people still have a little common sense. They can understand that a criminal should receive some form of retribution. So, when witnessing, I sometimes use an example of a murderer. I ask, "If your neighbor killed someone, would you want him roaming the streets or be locked up? A good judge wouldn't let him go free. What if the murderer promises never to kill again? Is that good enough?" Explain to the lost sinner that we are like spiritual criminals who are guilty of breaking God's laws. Like a judge in the courtroom has to pass judgment on a criminal, God has to punish sin.

Once again, this can be a sensitive subject. We must warn them about judgment to come, but we must try not to come across as judgmental. We want people to see that we are genuinely concerned for them and are trying to help. Our attitude can make all the difference in how our message is received. So, here are a few things you can say to help present pending judgment for sin:

You: "We have just seen that all men are sinners. Do you agree that you are guilty of sin?"

Sin Has to Be Punished

Friend: "Yes, but doesn't God forgive people?"

You: "He certainly does. We'll consider that soon, but first it is important to realize why we need forgiveness. What do you think happens to people who die with sin?"

Friend: "I'm not sure. Maybe miss out on going to Heaven."

You: "Yes, but that's not all. God has to punish sin."

Read: *"For the wages of sin is death; but the gift of God is eternal life through Jesus Christ our Lord"* (Romans 6:23).

You: "A wage is what we earn, and we have all earned death because of our sin. This is eternal death in a place called the Lake of Fire."

Read: *"And I saw a great white throne, and him that sat on it, from whose face the earth and the heaven fled away; and there was found no place for them. And I saw the dead, small and great, stand before God; and the books were opened: and another book was opened, which is the book of life: and the dead were judged out of those things which were written in the*

Simple Soulwinning Steps

> *books, according to their works"* (Revelation 20:11-12).

You: "This refers to the final judgment of sinners. Every lost person will be there, and their works will be judged out of God's record books. Those books are the evidence, and God is the Judge. When you stand before Him and He reads the evidence against you, will He say that you are innocent or guilty?"

Friend: "Unfortunately, He'd say that I'm guilty."

You: "What happens next in court? Sentencing."

Read: *"And death and hell were cast into the lake of fire. This is the second death"* (Revelation 20:14).

You: "The second death occurs when a soul is cast into the lake of fire to be punished for sin."

Friend: "That sounds pretty scary."

You: "It is. What would happen to you if you die with your sin?"

Friend: "Well, I hope I'd go to Heaven."

You: "God is the Judge, right?"

Fried: "Right."

Sin Has to Be Punished

You: "Is He a good Judge or a bad Judge?"

Friend: "A good One."

You: "Would a good judge in the courtroom allow a violent criminal go free?"

Friend: "No."

You: "We are like spiritual criminals who are guilty of breaking God's laws. Like a judge in the courtroom has to pass judgment on a criminal, God has to punish sin. So, when He sees all of your sins written in His books, are you guilty?"

Friend: "Yes."

Use the following verses to show that God punishes people for sin. In most cases, the first few verses will convince a person. However, more verses can be used to help those who are slow to accept it.

Verses for Showing the Judgment of Sin	
1. Romans 6:23	5. Luke 16:19-26
2. Romans 5:12	6. Isaiah 66:24
3. Revelation 20:12, 14	7. Psalm 9:17
4. Matthew 25:41	8. Luke 13:3

You: "What will happen to your soul if you are punished for your sin? [The person needs to

Simple Soulwinning Steps

                admit that they are in danger of eternal judgment if they are not forgiven.] That's not what you want, is it?"

Friend: "Absolutely not!"

You: "Because sin will bring us to the Lake of Fire, we need to find a way to be forgiven of our sins."

In the next lesson, we will see that many people believe they can escape judgment by doing good works. Sometimes we have to show the lost what can't save them before they are ready to accept Who can save them.

Please Note: Some people have a flippant attitude about hell. Occasionally, you might even encounter guys who boast that they are going to hell. They think it is a place where they will party with their friends and have a good time. If you run into this kind of an individual, make an effort to get him to see that hell is no joking matter. God's Word might sober them up. Some guys talk tough, but they are often afraid of what will happen when they die. Don't be intimidated. Take it as a challenge to help them. When they become belligerent or argumentative, you know it is time to politely end the conversation. Hopefully, you can at least leave them with a gospel tract.

Sin Has to Be Punished

Memory Challenge for Lesson 8

Memorize and recite the following verses:

Judgment – Romans 6:23
For the wages of sin is death; but the gift of God is eternal life through Jesus Christ our Lord.

_____   _____
Instructor's Signature   Date

Judgment – Revelation 20:14
And death and hell were cast into the lake of fire. This is the second death.

_____   _____
Instructor's Signature   Date

Additional Verses:

Verses	Instructor's Signature	Date
Revelation 20:15		
Romans 5:12		
Luke 13:3		
Psalm 9:17		

LESSON NINE

Good Works Do Not Save

In many cases, people will agree with you concerning what we discussed in the last two chapters. They acknowledge that they are sinners and that sinners will be punished. However, something illogical transpires in the hearts of many lost folks. Although they believe that they are sinners and that sinners go to hell, somehow they fail to realize that **they** will be punished for **their** sin. How could this be?

If people admit that they are sinners and that sinners go to hell, surely they should conclude that they will be punished for their sin. It's like one plus one equals two. However, we are not dealing with math. We are working with unregenerate hearts. What is obvious to us is not so clear to the lost because the heart of man is deceitful. Jeremiah reminds us, *"The heart is deceitful above all things, and desperately wicked: who can know it?"* (Jeremiah 17:9). That's why few people want to accept the fact that they will be judged for their sin.

Self-deceit often produces self-righteousness. A certain lawyer tempted Jesus with the question, *"Master, what shall I do to inherit eternal life?"* (Luke 10:25). Since he was trying to ensnare Christ, he likely

Simple Soulwinning Steps

had little interest in accepting His answer. Jesus directed him to the Scriptures, saying, *"What is written in the law? how readest thou?"* (Luke 10:26). Christ concluded that if a man kept the Law perfectly by loving God and his neighbor that he would live. Obviously, nobody can keep the Law to that extent, and that was Christ's point. Jesus confronted the man with his sin, but the lawyer did not want to own up to it because he was self-righteous. The account reveals this—*"But he, willing to justify himself, said unto Jesus, And who is my neighbour?"* (Luke 10:29). Like many religious people, the lawyer sought to justify himself. He wanted to look good and gloss over his sin.

When you realize that self-righteousness is a problem in most people, you will be more careful to address the matter when witnessing. You will come across people who may admit generally that they are sinners, but they do not want to accept that they are bad enough to go to hell. Their deceitful hearts lead them to defend themselves and look for ways to justify themselves. The bottom line with some people is that they do not want to admit that they are as bad as God says they are.

The job of the soulwinner is to carefully and compassionately show sinners the truth. Let's face it; most people think they are pretty good. Despite their sin, they want to believe that they will still go to Heaven because of all the good things they have done. It is the

Good Works Do Not Save

age-old belief that God has a set of scales in Heaven. They think that at the end of their lives, God will put all of their bad works on one side and all of their good works on the other. Because they have a high opinion of themselves, they think their goodness will tip the scales in their favor. This is called self-righteousness. We should not be too hard on people for thinking this way. After all, that is what most religions teach, and their deceitful heart wants to believe it. Many of us thought the same thing before we got saved. By showing some empathy, we can debunk the myth about scales in Heaven by sharing our testimony of how we believed the same thing before learning what the Bible says. This sets you up to share what the Scripture says. Ultimately, your goal is to show them the truth about their good works. Isaiah reveals that our good works are not so good after all. He explained that our righteous deeds are unacceptable in God's eyes. He said, *"But we are all as an unclean thing, and all our righteousnesses are as filthy rags"* (Isaiah 64:6). Compared to God, even our best works are dirty in His sight. That is why we need Christ's righteousness, not our own.

Again, this is a delicate matter, especially for religious people. Although we should not harshly accuse individuals of their self-righteousness, we must still show them that their good works will not exempt them from punishment. How do we do that? Consider the following approach:

Simple Soulwinning Steps

> **You:** "We have already seen that we are not righteous, and that sin will take us to hell. Somehow, we need to become righteous to go to Heaven. What do you think can make us righteous?"
>
> **Friend:** "I suppose being good. We should treat others like we would want to be treated. You know – don't hurt other people. Be nice."

You may get a variety of answers to the above question, but it usually boils down to people thinking that good works will save them: being kind to their neighbor, helping the unfortunate, going to church, getting baptized, keeping the Ten Commandments, or following Christ's example.

> **You:** "There are a lot of different churches out there. One says you have to get baptized to be righteous. Another teaches that you have to keep the Commandments. Some even say you have to speak in tongues. It's kind of confusing isn't it?
>
> **Friend:** "Sure is."
>
> **You:** "Let's see what the Bible says about good works."

Good Works Do Not Save

The chart below provides verses that show that good works cannot save. Use the verses that are appropriate for their situation. For example, if someone is trusting baptism to save him, start with that. Read enough verses to convince them. If someone thinks that the Ten Commandments (*"the law"*) will help save them, use the indicated verses to show otherwise. In most cases, you will focus on the column that deals with good works in general, especially when dealing with non-religious people. You must remember that people cannot be saved until they realize their works have no power to earn salvation.

Verses for Showing What Cannot Save People		
Ten Commandments	**Good Works**	**Baptism***
1. Acts 13:38-39	1. Ephesians 2:8-9	1. John 3:3-6
2. Romans 3:20, 28	2. Titus 3:5	2. Acts 2:41
3. Romans 10:3-4	3. Romans 3:12	3. Acts 8:36-37
4. Galatians 2:16, 21	4. Romans 4:1-7	4. 1 John 1:7
5. Galatians 3:10-11	5. Romans 11:6	5. Luke 7:37-50
6. Galatians 3:24-26	6. Isaiah 64:6	6. Luke 18:13-14
7. Galatians 5:4	7. Matthew 7:22-23	7. Luke 18:35-43
8. Philippians 3:9	8. 2 Timothy 1:9	8. Luke 23:39-43

*Some references for baptism show people who got saved without baptism!

Here is a sample of how you can continue the conversation with someone who is nominally religious.

Simple Soulwinning Steps

You: "Notice what Romans 3:20 teaches. No person is justified (made righteous) by following the Ten Commandments."

Read: *"Therefore by the deeds of the law there shall no flesh be justified in his sight: for by the law is the knowledge of sin"* (Romans 3:20).

Explain what the words in the verse mean: *deeds* – works, *law* – the Ten Commandments, *flesh* – person, *justified* – made righteous.

You: "So, nobody can be forgiven by keeping the Ten Commandments! Isn't it strange that churches teach us that we have to keep the Ten Commandments to be saved? That is actually the opposite of what the Bible teaches. When the teachings of religion contradict the Bible, which do you think we should believe?"

Friend: "The Bible."

Read: *"Therefore we conclude that a man is justified by faith without the deeds of the law"* (Romans 3:28).

You: "This verse clearly states that we are saved by faith without works. Salvation is not by believing and doing good works. It is by faith alone."

Good Works Do Not Save

If needed, you can use more verses from the chart above to prove that the Ten Commandments do not contribute to salvation.

Read: *"For by grace are ye saved through faith; and that not of yourselves: it is the gift of God: Not of works, lest any man should boast"* (Ephesians 2:8-9).

You: "Salvation is clearly *'not of works.'* It is a gift, and you never have to work for a gift. Someone else pays for the gift, and all we have to do is receive it. Jesus offers us eternal life as a free gift!"

In the next chapter, we will deal with an important requirement that must be met before someone can receive the free gift of salvation.

Simple Soulwinning Steps

Memory Challenge for Lesson 9

Memorize and recite the following verses:

Self-Righteousness – Romans 3:28
Therefore we conclude that a man is justified by faith without the deeds of the law.

_____   _____
Instructor's Signature   Date

Self-Righteousness – Ephesians 2:8-9
For by grace are ye saved through faith; and that not of yourselves: it is the gift of God: Not of works, lest any man should boast.

_____   _____
Instructor's Signature   Date

Additional Verses:

Verses	Instructor's Signature	Date
Romans 3:20		
Galatians 2:21		
Galatians 3:11		
Titus 3:5		

LESSON TEN

Repentance Is Required

Jesus made it clear that repentance is necessary for salvation. He told His audience, *"I tell you, Nay: but, except ye repent, ye shall all likewise perish"* (Luke 13:3). People who fail to repent will perish eternally. That is why soulwinners need to address judgment for sin and urge the lost to turn to Christ.

Jesus also commanded His disciples to include repentance in their preaching, saying, *"...that repentance and remission of sins should be preached in his name among all nations"* (Luke 24:47). It did not take Peter long to implement Christ's command. On the day of Pentecost, he confronted the Jews with their sin and their rejection of Jesus as the Messiah. Notice their response, *"Now when they heard this, they were pricked in their heart, and said unto Peter and to the rest of the apostles, Men and brethren, what shall we do?"* (Acts 2:37). The people were deeply convicted and wanted to know what they should do about their sin. The first word out of Peter's mouth was, *"Repent."* He told them what they needed to hear. What were the results? Three thousand souls repented and trusted Christ as

Savior! As we can see, the preaching of repentance is not only essential but also effective.

We do not get to pick and choose the message that we tell to others. If we are to be obedient disciples, we must proclaim repentance as Jesus commanded. However, we cannot simply tell a lost sinner to repent and expect that he knows what that means. We must understand what repentance is and learn how to explain it to others.

Confusion About Repentance

Unfortunately, there is much confusion about the subject of repentance both in the pulpit and the pew. Some preachers fail to preach repentance, others redefine it, and some teach that it is not necessary for salvation. I am not suggesting that all preachers who misunderstand repentance are malicious. Some are sincere, but instead of taking time to study the topic for themselves, they rely on what they have heard others say about it. I can testify that, like many other teachings in the Bible, my understanding of repentance has grown over the years. Thankfully, yours can too if necessary.

Since repentance is essential for salvation, we know that Satan works hard to prevent people from fully comprehending it. The devil also wants to stop Christians from calling people to repentance. Ultimately, his goal is to keep the lost in their sin and

Repentance Is Required

prevent them from turning to God for forgiveness. So, it is not surprising that people struggle with this doctrine. Thankfully, the Lord makes the matter clear through His Word, and we do not have to be intimidated by it.

It is vital for every soulwinner to learn what repentance is and to include it in his presentation of the gospel. Serious consequences can result if we either neglect or misunderstand repentance.

First, neglecting repentance can lead to false professions. This often occurs when soulwinners emphasize going to Heaven but fail to challenge the lost to deal with their sin. Salvation is not merely the act of asking Jesus to take you to Heaven when you die; it involves restoring the sinner's relationship with God. We should never invite people to receive Christ as Savior who are not convicted of their sin or fail to understand God's pending judgment for their sin.

Second, misunderstanding repentance can lead people to trust their works for salvation. Some churches teach that repentance requires a sinner to give up all of his sin in order to find favor with God and earn forgiveness. This is a horrible misconception! It is very similar to the Roman Catholic doctrine of penance, which teaches that sinners must make amends for their sinful actions. Man is not capable of making atonement for his own sins. That's why we need a Savior. Jesus did for us what we could not do for ourselves. Only He can make us righteous (See Romans 3:20-26, 2 Corinthians 5:21, Philippians 3:9). The Scriptures clearly teach that we are not saved by changing our ways and doing good deeds—*"Not by works of righteousness which we have done, but according to his mercy he saved us, by the washing of regeneration, and renewing of the Holy Ghost"* (Titus 3:5). Renewal of the soul is God's work at salvation, not man's work to secure salvation. We should not expect a lost sinner to transform his life in an attempt to be forgiven. Paul taught that a person's life changes after salvation—*"Therefore if any man be in Christ, he is a new creature: old things are passed away; behold, all things are become new"* (2 Corinthians 5:17). Be sure that you understand that salvation is by faith, not works (Ephesians 2:8-9).

Once again, let me remind you that Satan loves to create confusion. He wants us to either neglect or redefine repentance. If we do, the salvation of lost souls will be in jeopardy.

The Meaning of Repentance

The word *repent* is found in both the Old and New Testaments. Since words have meanings, it is wise to consider their definitions. Two Hebrew words found in the Old Testament, *nacham* and *shuwb*, are translated as *repent*. The first word refers to being sorrowful. The second word means "to turn back."[3] The children of Israel were often called to repent of their waywardness. God expected them to be sorry for their sin and turn back to Him. This teaches us that a proper attitude toward sin includes sorrow for wrong doing and turning to God.

The New Testament contains two main Greek words for the word *repent*. Like the Hebrew words, they also shed light on what it means to repent. The word used most frequently is *metanoeo*. It is primarily defined as "to think differently or afterwards."[4] This reveals that repentance involves a change of mind, usually after realizing wrongdoing. The word is further defined as "feeling compunction." *Compunction* is not a word we use much today, but its meaning is rich. It is defined as "A pricking of heart; poignant grief or remorse proceeding from a consciousness of guilt; the pain of sorrow or regret for having offended God, and incurred his wrath; the sting of conscience proceeding from a conviction of having violated a moral duty."[5] As you can see, repentance involves not only deep contemplation over one's actions but also contrition. Charles Spurgeon aptly said, "There is no repentance where a man can talk

---

[3] Strong, James, *Strong's Concordance*. Power BibleCD program by Online Publishing, Inc. by Phil Linder, 2000.
[4] Strong.
[5] Noah Webster, *Noah Webster's 1828 Dictionary of American English* (Franklin: e-Sword, 2000-2014), Digital Library.

lightly of sin, much less where he can speak tenderly and lovingly of it."[6] The second Greek word that is translated *repent* is *metamellomai*. It means "to care afterwards"[7] and can imply the idea of regret.

Perhaps the word meanings listed above are a bit overwhelming. Let's try to put them all together and come up with a working definition: "Repentance is a change of mind about sin which leads an individual to turn to God for forgiveness. It involves guilt, regret, and sorrow for sin." When witnessing to lost souls, it would be better to use a definition like this than to conduct a lengthy Hebrew and Greek word study. Keep it simple and practical.

The Sorrow of Repentance

When we considered the definition of *repentance*, we learned that it involves sorrow. However, not all sorrow involves repentance. When writing to the Corinthian believers, Paul discussed two kinds of sorrow: worldly sorrow and godly sorrow. Notice the result of each type of sorrow—*"For godly sorrow worketh repentance to salvation not to be repented of: but the sorrow of the world worketh death"* (2 Corinthians 7:10). Godly sorrow produces repentance, which leads the

---

[6] https://www.azquotes.com/author/13978-Charles_Spurgeon/tag/repentance, accessed 10/22/20.
[7] Strong.

Repentance Is Required

sinner to salvation. Worldly sorrow is unfruitful and ends in death. The difference between the two types of sorrow is described well by Dr. David Sorenson. He said, "The world regrets getting caught. Godly sorrow regrets the sin."[8] Showing remorse for sin is the key distinction.

Sorrow alone does not save someone. There are plenty of people who are sad about getting caught in their sin but have no desire to change their ways. Godly sorrow is quite different. It is a vital part of repentance. When speaking to the Corinthians, Paul said, *"Now I rejoice, not that ye were made sorry, but that ye sorrowed to repentance"* (2 Corinthians 7:9). Such sorrow produces heaviness in the heart. It is sobering. No one lightheartedly repents. They become serious about their sinful condition and sense an urgency to seek forgiveness from God.

Sometimes, people make a big mess of their lives and reap the terrible consequences of sin. They want their troubles to go away, but unfortunately, they often want to keep their sin. I have counseled people like this who have come forward during the invitation at church. I always ask people why they came forward. Many times they come seeking God's help, not His forgiveness. They just want a quick fix for their problems. Although I could probably get some people to pray the sinner's

---

[8] David Sorenson, *Understanding the Bible: I Corinthians through Philemon*, (Duluth: Northstar Ministries, 2008), 226.

Simple Soulwinning Steps

prayer by promising that all of their troubles would go away, that would be reckless. Instead, I try to get to the root of their problems by discussing God's judgment on sin and calling them to repentance. Far too often, people who are in great distress are not interested in listening to the gospel. Are they sorrowful? Oh, yes! Are they repentant? No. They suffer from what millions of others suffer from—*"the sorrow of the world."* Sadly, if they do not regret their sin more than their troubles, their lives will end in eternal death. This does not mean that such a person is hopeless. Their circumstances might get so bad that they will finally come to God on His terms. God's love and your concern may make a future witnessing opportunity fruitful.

Just because godly sorrow is part of repentance, it does not mean that people have to get choked up and weep over their sin in order to get saved. Some people shed tears, but many do not. Sorrow is a matter of the heart and is not always visible to the human eye. Rest assured that God sees a person's heart! So, don't always expect a great outward display of grief. Sorrow often leads to deep contemplation, resulting in a somber state. When you notice that a person becomes silent and serious about his sin, it is a good sign that he may be sorrowing to repentance.

Repentance Is Required

The Humility of Repentance

No one can be saved until he humbles himself before Almighty God. Notice what James said, *"God resisteth the proud, but giveth grace unto the humble"* (James 4:6). Pride is an offence to God. He hates it. He rejects it. He will not accept people who cling to their pride. The way to God is through humility. Because we are saved by grace, we must be humble in order to obtain that grace. Repentance can only come from a humble heart.

The story of the prodigal son provides a beautiful picture of repentance. The younger of the two sons demanded that his father give him his inheritance early. The father obliged, and the son wasted the money with a sinful lifestyle. When the money ran out, he humbled himself and returned with a repentant attitude. Take a moment and recall the account of his return home:

> *"And when he came to himself, he said, How many hired servants of my father's have bread enough and to spare, and I perish with hunger! I will arise and go to my father, and will say unto him, Father, I have sinned against heaven, and before thee, And am no more worthy to be called thy son: make me as one of thy hired servants. And he arose, and came to his father. But when he was yet a great way off, his father saw him,*

and had compassion, and ran, and fell on his neck, and kissed him. And the son said unto him, Father, I have sinned against heaven, and in thy sight, and am no more worthy to be called thy son. But the father said to his servants, Bring forth the best robe, and put it on him; and put a ring on his hand, and shoes on his feet: And bring hither the fatted calf, and kill it; and let us eat, and be merry: For this my son was dead, and is alive again; he was lost, and is found. And they began to be merry" (Luke 15:17-24).

Though the prodigal lived a loose life and dishonored his father, he *"came to himself"* and returned to his father in great humility. Notice that his repentance changed his demeanor. The son said, *"Father, I have sinned against heaven, and in thy sight, and am no more worthy to be called thy son."* He had previously demanded the privileges of a son. Afterward, he deemed himself unworthy to be a son.

When you witness to people, look for a humble attitude. Those who are haughty and arrogant toward God have not yet repented. When you find people in such a state, be patient and wait for them to respond to the Holy Spirit. They may not get saved the first time you witness to them, but in time they may humble themselves and repent. While serving as a missionary in Zambia, I witnessed to a young man named Obrien who

Repentance Is Required

was studying to become a Catholic priest. His older sister attended my church and had a burden for him to be saved. The first couple of times that I witnessed to him, he was very condescending in his responses. I can still visualize the smug, pompous look on his face as he belittled the true gospel message and insisted that baptism was necessary for salvation. In time, he softened a little, but he was still proud. After several weeks, I received a call from his sister. Obrien had become deathly sick, and she asked me to drive him to the hospital. He was so weak that he could not walk or talk. I was shocked when the hospital worker removed Obrien's shirt. His body was so emaciated that he looked like a skeleton wrapped in skin. He appeared to be another victim of HIV/AIDS. Knowing that I might never see him again, I went through the gospel one more time and pleaded with him to humble himself, admit he was wrong, and receive Christ as Savior. Since he could not speak, I led in a prayer, urging him to ask Jesus for forgiveness. I did not know if he made a decision or not. The hospital was so full that there were no available beds. Shortly after they placed him on a mat on the floor, I said what I figured was my final good bye. To our surprise, after a few days he gained enough strength to leave the hospital. Everyone was happy, but there was even better news than that. He told his sister that he had received Christ the night I witnessed to him in the hospital!

Simple Soulwinning Steps

Obrien was still not well. So, his family took him back to the village. When lost family members tried to take him to the witchdoctor, he refused because he had become a Christian. Shortly thereafter, he passed away, but he died as a saved man. Like the prodigal son, Obrien did not repent until his attitude changed. You also may encounter people who are too proud to repent. Be patient and continue to help those who *"oppose themselves; if God peradventure will give them repentance to the acknowledging of the truth"* (2 Timothy 2:25).

Realms of Repentance

As we have seen, if there is no change of mind about sin, there is no repentance. If there is no repentance, there is no salvation. We stated that repentance involves a change of mind. But what does a sinner need to change his mind about?

First, sinners must think differently about sin. They must change their mind about their sin, express sorrow for it, and desire to be changed. Then, by faith, they must look to Christ to make those changes, acknowledging that they are powerless to save themselves.

Years ago my wife and I witnessed to a young lady who had attended church occasionally while growing up. She had become a lesbian and wanted to talk to us about it. Though she admitted that she needed Jesus, she tried to justify her actions and dismiss her sin. If we had told her that all she needed to do was pray and ask Jesus to take her to Heaven when she died, she probably would have readily done so. However, she was not repentant. She had not seen her sin as God saw it and had no desire to change. She wanted peace with God but also wanted to continue in sin at the same time. Although she was miserable because of God's conviction, she was unwilling to repent. It was sad to see her refuse God's offer of salvation. Thankfully, years later she acknowledged her sin and turned to Christ for salvation. After she was saved, her lifestyle changed. The lesson to learn from this is that when people stubbornly defend wickedness, they are not ready to be saved.

Secondly, sinners must think differently about the Savior. They must see Jesus as their only hope of forgiveness. Sadly, most religions teach some form of a works-based salvation in which followers are expected to perform many good deeds in order to earn salvation. However, Paul taught a clear distinction between faith in Christ and faith in one's works. He said, *"Therefore we conclude that a man is justified by faith without the deeds of the law"* (Romans 3:28). Charles Spurgeon stated this well, "I look away from self, and sin, and all

Simple Soulwinning Steps

idea of personal merit, and I trust the Lord Jesus as the Savior whom God has given."[9]

My wife's aunt was a nun in the Roman Catholic Church for over sixty years. Our family was able to visit her one day, and she was thrilled to see us, especially our children. After a little tour of her place, we took her to a restaurant for a nice meal. Our main purpose for visiting was to present the gospel to her. After dinner, I began to compassionately share that faith in Jesus, not in our works, secures salvation. Her eyes were like windows to her soul. I could see deep conviction as she realized that what she had been taught for decades was not true. She had trusted the wrong thing for salvation, and she knew it. Her eyes began to water, but before a tear was shed, her countenance quickly changed. It was as if she had closed the door to her heart. She was unwilling to repent of her self-righteousness. Though my wife corresponded with her for a while, her aunt seemed distant. In time, all communication ceased and we learned that she had passed away. As far as we know, she never repented. False religion blinds the hearts of many kind-hearted, sacrificial people.

To recap, sinners must repent of two things. They need to change their minds about sin and desire God more than their sin. Then, they must change their

---

[9] Charles H. Spurgeon, *Faith's Checkbook* (Chicago: Moody Press, 1992), 136.

Repentance Is Required

minds about the Savior and realize that He is the only hope of salvation.

The Counterpart of Repentance

Although repentance is required for salvation, it is not enough to save someone. It must be accompanied by faith. Jesus preached at the onset of His ministry, saying, *"The time is fulfilled, and the kingdom of God is at hand: repent ye, and believe the gospel"* (Mark 1:15). Notice that He made two demands: repent and believe the gospel. In addition to repenting, the lost must *"believe the gospel."* The word *believe* refers to exercising faith. After a sinner changes his mind about his sin, he must turn to Christ and trust Him for forgiveness. Sorrow is not enough. Repentance is not enough. Faith in Christ must follow. The Bible repeatedly states that salvation is by faith. The natural result of true repentance is faith.

An eighteen-wheeler is composed of a truck and trailer. The truck leads, and the trailer follows right behind it. Salvation is similar. Repentance leads the way, and faith immediately follows. If there is no trailer attached to the truck, you do not have an eighteen-wheeler. Likewise, if you have repentance without faith, there is no salvation.

Simple Soulwinning Steps

The Presentation of Repentance

After reading so much about repentance, you may be thinking, "This is a lot of material. How do I present all of that to a lost person?" Don't worry. You don't necessarily need to present a long, drawn-out theology lesson about repentance. Neither do you have to be a Bible scholar to talk about it with the unsaved. My goal for elaborating on the topic in this chapter was not to overwhelm anyone. My intent was two-fold. First, I wanted to compel soulwinners to include repentance in their gospel presentation. Second, I wanted to provide a solid foundation on the subject. In order to explain repentance properly to the lost, we must know what it is. Thankfully, we do not have to teach everything we know about the subject!

Here are some basic things to cover. Ensure that people understand that their sin will be judged. They should have a change of mind about their sin and the Savior. In order to be saved, they must be sorry for their sin, turn to Jesus for forgiveness, and desire a changed life. They should trust Jesus to do for them what they cannot do for themselves. This means that they trust Jesus to make them righteous, not their good works. Jesus made it clear that repentance and faith work together. He said, *"...repent ye, and believe the gospel"* (Mark 1:15). When people change their minds about their sin and trust Jesus to forgive them, they are saved.

Repentance Is Required

It is that simple. God did not make the plan of salvation complicated.

In previous lessons, we discussed presenting the fact of sin, the judgment of sin, and the inability of good works to atone for sin. Listed below are some ideas for presenting repentance:

You: "As we have seen, God hates sin. What should our attitude be towards sin?"

Friend: "We should hate it too."

You: "Jesus told us what would happen if we failed to deal with our sin."

Read: "*I tell you, Nay: but, except ye repent, ye shall all likewise perish*" (Luke 13:3).

You: "The word *repent* means 'to have a change of mind.' God wants us to think differently about our sin. We must see how bad it really is and what it will cost us in the end. If we fail to repent, we will perish. Can you guess what that means?"

Friend: "It means to die, right?"

You: "Yes, it refers to death—spiritual death. When a person perishes, his soul is cast into the lake of fire and is punished forever. God doesn't want us to go there. That is why He

Simple Soulwinning Steps

tells us to repent. What happens if you fail to repent?"

Friend: "God would punish me for my sin."

You: "Let me explain repentance a little more. [Use the working definition we discussed earlier in the lesson.] Repentance is a change of mind about sin which leads us to turn to God for forgiveness. If you feel guilty about your sin and are sorry for your actions, God is willing to forgive you. Has sin helped or hurt your relationship with God?"

Friend: "It has definitely hurt it."

You: "As we already saw, we can't make ourselves righteous by doing good works. Only Jesus can change us and make us good enough for Heaven. That's where faith comes in."

Read: Jesus said, *"...repent ye, and believe the gospel"* (Mark 1:15).

You: "God expects us to change our minds about our sin, turn to Jesus, and believe the gospel for forgiveness. [Explain that the gospel refers to the death, burial, and resurrection.] The word *believe* means to depend on Christ's work on the cross for salvation, not our works. Do you want God to forgive you and change

Repentance Is Required

your life?"

Friend: "Yes. I need that."

You: "Let's see a little bit more about what Jesus did on the cross for us."

Never forget that God *"commandeth all men every where to repent"* (Acts 17:30). If people need to repent, they must be urged to do so. Hopefully, you are now well prepared to explain repentance! In the next lesson, we will discuss the substitution of Christ for our sin and give some tips on explaining it to the lost.

Simple Soulwinning Steps

Memory Challenge for Lesson 10

Memorize and recite the following verses:

Repentance – Luke 13:3
I tell you, Nay: but, except ye repent, ye shall all likewise perish.

_____   _____

Instructor's Signature   Date

Repentance – Mark 1:15
... The time is fulfilled, and the kingdom of God is at hand: repent ye, and believe the gospel.

_____   _____

Instructor's Signature   Date

Additional Verses:

Verses	Instructor's Signature	Date
2 Corinthians 7:10		
Acts 2:38		
Luke 24:47		
Mark 6:12		

LESSON ELEVEN

Jesus Took Our Place

The gospel is good news. In fact, it is the best news a person can ever hear! However, most people are not ready to accept the good news until they are convicted of their sin. After we have presented the bad news about sin to the lost, we can share the good news about the Savior. When we get to this part of the soulwinning presentation, it is natural for our demeanors to change. After all, our message changes from doom to hope. As the sun appears brighter to the individual who has just walked out of a dark room, Jesus radiates more to the soul whose conscience has been awakened to sin.

The exciting doctrine that we get to present to the convicted sinner is substitution. No, you do not have to use the word *substitution* when you witness. Simply explain the concept. It is simple—Jesus died in our place, taking the punishment of our sins upon Himself so that He could offer us His righteousness.

Peter explained substitution this way, *"For Christ also hath once suffered for sins, the just for the unjust, that he might bring us to God, being put to death in the flesh, but quickened by the Spirit"* (1 Peter 3:18). Notice that sin had to be punished, and Jesus *"suffered for sins."* Those sins were not His sins because He was sinless; they were our sins. His sacrifice was *"the just for the unjust."* That indicates substitution. Webster defined *substitution* as, "The act of putting one person or thing in the place of another to supply its place."[10] Clearly Jesus took our place on the cross. We deserve to be punished because we are unjust. However, because He was just, His sacrifice was sufficient to appease the wrath of God against sin.

To help the lost to understand substitution, I often use an illustration that most people can relate to. I explain that a substitute teacher takes the place of a teacher when the teacher is not able to do the job. Clearly, we are not able to pay for our sins with our good works. We need a Substitute to do for us what we cannot do for ourselves. This is where Christ steps in. His sacrifice was a perfect work, and God accepted Christ's payment for sin.

Paul provides a clear description of substitution, *"For he* [God] *hath made him* [Christ] *to be sin for us, who knew no sin; that we might be made the righteousness of God in him"* (2 Corinthians 5:21). Jesus took our sin upon Himself so that we can have His righteousness. Before our salvation, we had no righteousness, but through faith in Christ our sin is replaced by the righteousness of Jesus. What a Substitute He is!

---

[10] Webster.

Jesus Took Our Place

Receiving Christ as Substitute is the result of repentance. As we have already seen, to repent means to have a change of mind. A sinner must change his mind about his sin, acknowledge that his good works are unable to save him, and turn to Christ to make him righteous. When this happens, it is often visibly noticeable. It is as if a light bulb turned on in their hearts and illuminated their darkened understanding. Suddenly, they see the truth! They may even say, "Oh, now I get it!" Regardless of how people express their realization, your job is to ensure that they have changed their mind about their sin and their good works. Then, you lead them to trust Christ.

At this point in the gospel presentation, you want to stress two things. First, you must show how Jesus took their place on the cross. Their sins were placed upon Christ (Isaiah 53:6). Second, reiterate that it is only by trusting Jesus, not their works, that they can be saved.

The following chart contains Scriptures that you can use to explain substitution.

Verses for Showing Substitution	
1. Romans 5:6, 8	3. 2 Corinthians 5:21
2. Isaiah 53:6	4. 1 Peter 3:18

Here is a possible way to continue your gospel presentation:

Simple Soulwinning Steps

You: "We have seen that we are all sinners, and if we fail to repent, we will face eternal punishment. That was the bad news. Are you ready for some good news?

Friend: "Oh, yes. I certainly would."

You: "Although we can't make ourselves righteous, Jesus can. We have sin but no righteousness. Jesus has righteousness but no sin. When He died on the cross, He took your place and was punished for your sins. Your sins have already been paid for, but you must accept Christ as your Savior to become righteous."

Read: *"All we like sheep have gone astray; we have turned every one to his own way; and the LORD hath laid on him the iniquity of us all"* (Isaiah 53:6).

You: "All of our sins were put on Jesus! Did you ever have a substitute teacher?"

Friend: "Lots of them."

You: "What do substitute teachers do?"

Friend: "They fill in for the teacher."

You: "Right. They take the place of the teacher when the teacher is not up to working. In like manner, we are not up to the task of saving

Jesus Took Our Place

ourselves. So, Jesus stepped in as our Substitute! He did what we could not do; He paid for our sins!"

Read: *"But God commendeth his love toward us, in that, while we were yet sinners, Christ died for us"* (Romans 5:8).

You: "This verse shows that Jesus died for us, meaning in our place. The next verse really makes it clear."

Read: *"For he* [God] *hath made him* [Jesus] *to be sin for us, who knew no sin; that we might be made the righteousness of God in him"* (2 Corinthians 5:21).

You: "Jesus became sin for us so that we could have His righteousness. He took our place. His work saves, not ours! When we receive Him, we get rid of what keeps us out of Heaven (our sin) and receive what is needed to get into Heaven (His righteousness). Do you need Jesus' righteousness, or do you think you can get into Heaven the way you are?"

Friend: "According to what you have showed me from the Bible, I'm not good enough to get into Heaven. I need Jesus."

Simple Soulwinning Steps

You: "That's right. We all do! Let's look at a few verses from the Gospel of John which discuss eternal life. Notice that none of the verses mention doing good things, getting baptized, or keeping the Ten Commandments to be saved. In fact, every verse has the same message: we need to trust Jesus to be saved."

Read: At this point, read a few of the following verses and show that salvation is only by faith in Jesus: John 1:12, 3:16, 3:36, 5:24, 6:47, 10:9, 11:25-26, 14:6, and 20:31.

You: "Jesus died, was buried, and rose again for you?"

Read: *"That if thou shalt confess with thy mouth the Lord Jesus, and shalt believe in thine heart that God hath raised him from the dead, thou shalt be saved. For with the heart man believeth unto righteousness; and with the mouth confession is made unto salvation"* (Romans 10:9-10).

You: "Do you believe that Jesus did that for you?"

Friend: "Yes."

You: "That means that you can be saved!"

Jesus Took Our Place

Memory Challenge for Lesson 11

Memorize and recite the following verses:

Substitution – Romans 5:8
But God commendeth his love toward us, in that, while we were yet sinners, Christ died for us.

_____   _____
Instructor's Signature   Date

Substitution – 2 Corinthians 5:21
For he hath made him to be sin for us, who knew no sin; that we might be made the righteousness of God in him.

_____   _____
Instructor's Signature   Date

Additional Verses:

Verses	Instructor's Signature	Date
John 6:47		
John 10:9		
John 14: 6		
1 Peter 3:18		

LESSON TWELVE

We Must Trust Jesus

After giving a clear presentation of the gospel, what's left? The sinner must now act upon what he knows. Consider the following illustration. When a person enters a dark room, he knows that if he flips the light switch that the light will come on. However, the light won't come on until he flips the switch! Likewise, a person may know that he needs to receive Jesus, but he is not saved until he does so. When someone understands the gospel, you can urge him to trust Christ. However, you should not push him to pray a "sinner's prayer" if he is not ready or repentant.

When going shopping, few things are worse than encountering a pushy salesman. Some salesmen do their best to sell a product to you that you neither want nor need. Unfortunately, some preachers train soulwinners to be a lot like salesmen. They suggest using tricky tactics to coerce people to pray a prayer. Like an unsuspecting customer who buys a product that he had no intention of purchasing, lost sinners are led to pray a prayer for salvation who express little to no interest in the gospel. That is manipulation, not salvation! Such "soulwinners" are more despicable than

Simple Soulwinning Steps

unscrupulous salesmen because they pronounce people to be saved who have neither repented nor exercised faith. We should never use such tactics.

Some preachers may argue that we should do whatever is necessary to get someone to pray because they think that prayer saves. They may even quote Scripture such as Romans 10:13 to back up their claim— *"For whosoever shall call upon the name of the Lord shall be saved."* However, taken in context, we know that this passage does not teach that prayer alone saves. A few verses before this verse, we see that faith in Christ is necessary, *"That if thou shalt confess with thy mouth the Lord Jesus, and shalt **believe in thine heart** that God hath raised him from the dead, thou shalt be saved. For with the heart man **believeth unto righteousness**; and with the mouth confession is made unto salvation"* (Romans 10:9-10 – emphasis added). Clearly, praying a prayer without faith does not save. Salvation is a matter of the heart, not merely of the lips.

Although we should not be pushy or manipulative, there is one valuable lesson that we can learn from salesmen. A good salesman will present his product and determine if the customer needs or wants it. If so, he asks for the order. What kind of salesman would make a convincing case for his product, see the customer ready to buy, and then walk away? As a salesman asks customers if they are ready to make a purchase, soulwinners must learn to ask sinners if they are ready

We Must Trust Jesus

to receive Jesus. They need salvation, and we must ask if they want it. Obviously, we should only invite people to accept Christ who have shown regret for their sin and express an understanding that salvation is by faith.

When Christ called some of His disciples, He said, *"Follow me, and I will make you fishers of men"* (Matthew 4:19). Instead of catching fish, Jesus said, *"...from henceforth thou shalt catch men"* (Luke 5:10). How would they catch men? As fishermen, they understood that once fish entered their net, they had to draw the net. In other words, they had to try to catch them before they got away. When we witness to people who seem ready to be saved, we should not let them go without trying to rescue them from the depths of sin. Here are some ideas that will help you to know when and how to draw the net.

Determine

It is the soulwinner's job to discern whether or not the sinner is ready to be saved. You must lean upon the Holy Spirit's guidance to see if the person that you are witnessing to really understands and is ready. If I have any doubts about whether or not the person is truly sincere, I typically ask, "We have been talking for quite a while already. Would you like me to continue to explain how you can receive Jesus, or would you like me to come back another time?"

Simple Soulwinning Steps

Sometimes people will say, "Yes, maybe you could come back another time." This often indicates that they are either not very interested or that they are preoccupied with something else. Hopefully, they will be more eager to listen when you follow up on them.

The majority of time I ask the above question, I get a positive response. I have even had people emphatically say something like, "This is important. I need to hear how to be saved now, not later." When people want to hear more of the gospel, it is a good sign that they may be close to making a decision to trust Christ.

Explain

When someone is ready to be saved, I usually try to draw the net in a similar way as follows:

You: "Let's review what we have learned so far. God loves you, but how does He feel about your sin?"

Friend: "He hates it."

You: "Can you go to Heaven with your sin?"

Friend: "No."

You: "Can you save yourself by doing good works?"

Friend: "No. You showed me that good works do not save anyone."

We Must Trust Jesus

You: "Right! So, Who can save you?"

Friend: "Jesus."

You: "Would you like to be saved?"

Friend: "Most definitely."

You: "Here's how you can receive Jesus as your Savior. Jesus gave us a simple illustration."

Read: He said, *"Behold, I stand at the door, and knock: if any man hear my voice, and open the door, I will come in to him"* (Revelation 3:20).

You: "If I went to your house, could I enter if the door is closed?"

Friend: "No."

You: "I would have to knock or ask if anyone was home. I could not come in until you open the door and invite me inside. In the same way, Jesus is waiting at the door to your life and wants to come in, but He can't enter until you invite Him. Would you like to open the door to your life and ask Jesus to come in?"

Friend: "Yes, I would."

You: "Here's how you can open the door."

Simple Soulwinning Steps

Read: *"For whosoever shall call upon the name of the Lord shall be saved"* (Romans 10:13).

You: "Simply call on the name of Jesus in faith, and you **shall** be saved. It is a certainty—not just a possibility. Does God lie?"

Friend: "No."

You: "Simply ask Him to come into your life and be your Savior! You can ask Jesus right now. Would you like to do that?"

Friend: "Yes, I would."

You: "Jesus wants to hear something like this: *'Dear Jesus, I know that I have sinned against You and deserve to be punished. I am sorry for my sin and realize that I cannot save myself by doing good works. Please come into my life, save me, and change me. Right now, I receive You as my Savior. Thank You for saving me. Amen.'* Does that prayer express the desire of your heart?"

Friend: "Yes, it does."

You: "Would you like to pray something like that to God on your own, or would you like me to help you with a prayer?"

Some people have never prayed before and may feel intimidated by being around an "experienced" believer.

We Must Trust Jesus

Explain that God is more concerned with their faith than He is about the exact wording of their prayer. Urge them to pray from their hearts. If someone needs help with a prayer, stress the following:

You: "My prayer cannot save you, but I will help you with the words as you pray to Jesus. Picture the Lord in Heaven and talk to Him as you pray after me."

At this point, you can lead the person phrase by phrase in a prayer for salvation. Both of you should pray aloud. To ensure the person prays aloud, try saying something like:

You: "I will pray a little bit, and when I hear you pray, I will continue."

What If Someone Does Not Pray?

Sometimes people decide not to receive the Lord even after you thought that they were ready to be saved. This can happen for a number of reasons. Let's consider a few possibilities:

1. They are not ready to repent. Although they want to go to Heaven, they are not ready to deal with their sin. They may have counted the cost and do not want Christ to change their lives yet.

Simple Soulwinning Steps

2. They think their sin is too great and are doubtful that God would forgive them. Some people think that they are a lost cause and have no hope.
3. They still have questions and do not feel ready. It can be difficult for religious people to give up what they have been taught all of their lives. Sometimes they want more time to think about it and be sure that what you are telling them is the truth.
4. They are shy and want to pray at home or in private.

So, what do you do when people decide not to pray? First of all, show concern. Don't get upset or frustrated. Second, ask them why they are not ready to receive the Lord. Their answer will help you determine what step to take next. You may have to reassure them of God's love, answer an important question, or gently warn them of the dangers of delaying.

The Lord may lead you to urge someone to reconsider. Remind people that God has an accepted time to be saved—*"I have heard thee in a time accepted, and in the day of salvation have I succoured thee: behold, now is the accepted time; behold, now is the day of salvation"* (2 Corinthians 6:2). However, you do not want people to pray a prayer just to get you leave them alone. You must have discernment to know how to proceed. At the minimum, you should give people a

We Must Trust Jesus

good tract and encourage them to read it before the day is over. Urge them to put their faith in Christ, and remind them that God will remove their heavy load of sin once they do. Then, assure them that you are available to answer any questions and want to help in any way possible. If possible, follow up with them within a few days.

Do not get discouraged when people do not get saved. You may be one of many people that God will use to reach them. Paul reminds us that some plant the seed of the Word of God and others water that seed with a further witness, but God is ultimately the One Who brings the harvest (1 Corinthians 3:6). Have faith that the Word that you share with others will continue to work in their hearts. Claim God's promise, *"So shall my word be that goeth forth out of my mouth: it shall not return unto me void, but it shall accomplish that which I please, and it shall prosper in the thing whereto I sent it"* (Isaiah 55:11).

If someone does not get saved after you witness to them, try not to second guess yourself. It is easy to say in hindsight, "Oh, if I had only shared one more verse it may have made a difference." If you presented the truth and did your best, pray and leave it in God's hands. Take comfort in knowing that God does not give up on people easily. He loves them too much for that.

My father-in-law told me about a man who he had witnessed to at work decades ago. The man did not get

Simple Soulwinning Steps

saved at the time, but many years later he did. When he told my father-in-law, it was a real blessing to him. His labor was not in vain! God had, in fact, used his witness. The seed that we sow today may take a while to bear fruit, but we should not get discouraged. What a blessing it will be when we get to Heaven and meet people who got saved long after we had witnessed to them! Never lose hope in your soulwinning efforts.

We Must Trust Jesus

Memory Challenge for Lesson 12

Memorize and recite the following verses:

Solution – Revelation 3:20
Behold, I stand at the door, and knock: if any man hear my voice, and open the door, I will come in to him, and will sup with him, and he with me.

_____   _____
Instructor's Signature   Date

Solution – Romans 10:13
For whosoever shall call upon the name of the Lord shall be saved.

_____   _____
Instructor's Signature   Date

Additional Verses:

Verses	Instructor's Signature	Date
Romans 10:9		
John 1:12		
John 6:37		
Revelation 22:17		

LESSON THIRTEEN

Salvation Is Forever

When a person repents and receives Jesus as Savior, it is an exciting occasion! Jesus said, *"...there is joy in the presence of the angels of God over one sinner that repenteth"* (Luke 15:10). God is happy, the one who is saved is happy, and you are happy to have a part in it.

So much occurs when people get saved. They are cleansed, forgiven, regenerated, justified, sanctified, indwelt by the Holy Spirit, adopted into God's family, and given eternal life. Of course, a new convert does not understand everything that has happened to him, but he does realize that things are different.

One of the first things that you must teach a new believer is the matter of eternal security. All saved people are eternally secure. They can never go to hell because salvation is forever. Eternal security was a clear teaching of Christ and His followers. Consider just a few examples:

1. Jesus said, *"My sheep hear my voice, and I know them, and they follow me: And I give unto them eternal life; and they shall never perish, neither*

Simple Soulwinning Steps

shall any man pluck them out of my hand" (John 10:27-28). God immediately gives eternal life to every sinner who trusts Christ for salvation. Since it is eternal, it cannot stop. Notice that Jesus did not say, "I **will** give unto them eternal life." He said, *"I give unto them eternal life."* Everlasting life is not something we receive in the future. We have it already! Since new converts already possess eternal life, they need to understand that *"they shall never perish."*

2. Paul assured us that the soul of every believer is sealed and secure. He said, *"And grieve not the holy Spirit of God, whereby ye are sealed unto the day of redemption"* (Ephesians 4:30). The seal used by the Romans in Paul's day was backed by the authority of Rome. Something that was sealed was not to be tampered with. When God sets His seal upon a soul, it is safe and protected. No one can tamper with the eternal life that Christ gave to us. God the Holy Spirit stands as Guardian of our souls.

3. Peter taught that Christians have *"an inheritance incorruptible, and undefiled, and that fadeth not away, reserved in heaven"* (1 Peter 1:4). Further, he said that we are *"kept by the power of God"* (1 Peter 1:5). What a blessing to know that we

have a home that is reserved in Heaven and that God's great power keeps us saved so that we will one day enjoy our promised inheritance!

4. Jude said that Christians are *"sanctified by God the Father, and preserved in Jesus Christ"* (Jude 1). Sanctification refers to holiness. God is the One Who makes us holy. Therefore, we depend on His finished work on the cross to save us and keep us saved. The word *preserved* is a military term that means "to guard." Praise God that He not only saves us but also protects our salvation!

Although every Christian's eternity is sealed and secured, not all believers realize it. For example, a new believer may be on cloud nine initially after getting saved. His burden of sin is gone, and he has peace that he never had before. However, he will soon discover that his sinful flesh is prone to stumble. He may think that he needs to get saved again each time he sins. Without understanding the doctrine of eternal security, he may not know from day to day if he is even a child of God. This uncertainty can lead to confusion, fear, and a loss of joy. Every new convert needs further instruction. This is where you come in. Here are a couple of tips to follow after someone makes a decision for salvation.

Simple Soulwinning Steps

Review

After people receive Christ as Savior, verify that they understood the gospel. I never tell a person that he is saved just because he prayed a prayer. Here's how I typically converse with someone who has just prayed to be saved:

You: "If you died right now, where would you go?"

Friend: "Heaven."

Sometimes people say it confidently, while other times people show a little hesitancy, and reply with a quesiton, "Heaven?" When people seem unsure about whether or not they are now saved, it is important to review the promises that God makes about salvation. I often use Romans 10:13—*"For whosoever shall call upon the name of the Lord shall be saved."* I typically stress the words *"shall be saved."* This shows that it is guaranteed, not iffy. If doubts linger, the person may not have fully understood the gospel. At this point, it is wise to review the verses that teach salvation is by faith, not works. You do not want to give assurance of salvation to someone who is not saved!

If the person has answered correctly and confidently, I continue as follows:

You: "Why would you go to Heaven?"

Salvation Is Forever

How the person answers this question will give you an idea of what he has trusted to save him. You are looking for responses like, "I have received Jesus," "I asked Jesus to save me," or "I invited Jesus into my life."

What if the individual gives a wrong answer? He may say something like, "I believe in Jesus and am going to follow His ways." If you get this kind of response, decide if he needs to hear more verses that teach salvation is by faith, not works. It may be that he didn't understand that salvation is by faith alone, or he possibly just got his terms mixed up. What he may have meant was that he trusted Jesus and was determined to live for Him now. That is actually a good answer!

Remember, we are not there to interrogate but to help! So, don't be harsh or critical if someone fails to give you exactly the right answers. After all, new believers are not Bible scholars! Be kind and patient. If necessary, you may have to return another day and go through the plan of salvation again to properly assess his spiritual state. At such a follow-up visit, it is usually clear whether or not the person actually got saved.

It has been my experience that when people get saved, there will be some evidence of it. The new convert might be relieved, happy, or burdened for lost loved ones. If someone is saved, there will definitely be some sort of change in his life—*"Therefore if any man be in Christ, he is a new creature: old things are passed*

Simple Soulwinning Steps

away; behold, all things are become new" (2 Corinthians 5:17).

When people demonstrate a proper understanding of salvation, you can proceed to share verses about eternal security. We will discuss that next.

Equip

It is important to understand that eternal security and assurance of salvation are not the same things. Every born-again Christian possesses eternal security, but not all are assured they have it. It is the job of the soulwinner to provide assurance by explaining eternal security.

Satan is not pleased when he loses souls to the Lord. Therefore, he tries to get Christians to doubt their salvation. By arming our new brethren with Scripture, they will be able to fend off the attacks of the devil. Rather than pronouncing people as saved, allow the Holy Spirit to use His Word to bring that assurance. As I stated earlier, I do not tell people that they are saved just because they have prayed. Plenty of people pray without faith, and we don't want to give assurance to someone who is not saved. To avoid this, I like to use qualifying statements like, "If you received Jesus, then...." Here are some suggestions of what you might say next:

Salvation Is Forever

You: "Did you receive Jesus?"

Friend: "Yes, I did."

You: "Let's see what the Bible says about those who receive Him."

Read: *"But as many as received him, to them gave he power to become the sons of God, even to them that believe on his name"* (John 1:12).

You: "**If you received Him**, what did you become?"

Friend: "Well, according to that verse, I became a son of God."

You: "**If you believed on His name**, you are now one of His children, and His children get to live with Him in Heaven for eternity."

Read: *"My sheep hear my voice, and I know them, and they follow me: And I give unto them eternal life; and they shall never perish, neither shall any man pluck them out of my hand"* (John 10:27-28).

You: "Jesus calls those who are saved His sheep. Notice that He gives them eternal life. What does *eternal* mean?"

Friend: "Forever."

You: "Right. It is something that lasts forever. So,

Simple Soulwinning Steps

if you are saved, you have life that can never stop. Look at the words, *"they shall never perish."* What does the word *never* mean?

Friend: "Uh...never means never."

You: "Exactly. It means "not ever, absolutely not." **If you are saved**, you cannot possibly perish in hell. The reason is because Jesus has you in His hand, and nobody, including yourself, can get you out of His hand. Jesus not only saves us but keeps us saved! So, can you ever lose your salvation?"

Friend: "I guess not."

You: "You might wonder what happens if you sin after getting saved. We just saw that you can't lose your salvation. However, you can lose your fellowship with God. If you want to stay close to the Lord and enjoy His blessings, you have to confess your sins daily."

You: "Let me explain it another way. Are children always obedient?"

Friend: "Certainly not."

You: "If a boy is disobedient, does he stop being a son?"

Friend: "No."

You: "Exactly. In the same way, as children of God we sometimes obey Him and at other times disobey Him. God doesn't kick us out of His family when we disobey. No good father would do that! When we're obedient, we are blessed; when we're disobedient, we are chastened. You determine how God deals with you. So, start doing right!"

Simple Soulwinning Steps

Memory Challenge for Lesson 13

Memorize and recite the following verses:

Security – John 10:27
My sheep hear my voice, and I know them, and they follow me:

_____   _____
Instructor's Signature   Date

Security – John 10:28
And I give unto them eternal life; and they shall never perish, neither shall any man pluck them out of my hand.

_____   _____
Instructor's Signature   Date

Additional Verses:

Verses	Instructor's Signature	Date
1 John 5:13		
John 5:24		
Jude 24		
Philippians 1:6		

LESSON FOURTEEN

There Is Much to Learn

When you lead someone to the Lord, you will be very excited. In your zeal, you may want to tell him everything that you know about the Christian life, but keep your enthusiasm in check. This is not the time for a long Bible study. You do not want to overload new converts with too much information. After all, people can only absorb a limited amount of information at a time. Besides, we must be sensitive to people's schedules. If you carelessly monopolize their time, they may hesitate to meet with you again. Your main goal at this point in the conversation is to briefly encourage the new believer and line up a future visit so that you can begin to disciple him.

Encourage

In some cases, you may not have much time to do follow-up work. If time permits, explain that salvation changes people. New believers may struggle to realize how God works to make them more like Jesus unless you tell them. Then, challenge new converts to take steps to grow in their faith. This naturally opens the

Simple Soulwinning Steps

door for you to request a follow-up visit. Try wrapping up your conversation like this:

You: "Before I go, let me quickly share with you a couple of things that might be helpful to you."

Read: *"Therefore if any man be in Christ, he is a new creature: old things are passed away; behold, all things are become new."* (2 Corinthians 5:17).

You: "Once we get saved, our lives begin to change. When do you think those changes should start?"

Friend: "Right away."

It is important to get new converts to see that God expects them to change. It is especially helpful when they acknowledge that those changes should begin right away. This will help them to understand why they have a new sensitivity to sin and a desire to please God.

You: "As you have seen, the Bible is a big Book, and there are many more lessons to learn. God wants you to take steps to grow in your Christian life."

Read: *"As newborn babes, desire the sincere milk of the word, that ye may grow thereby"* (1 Peter 2:2).

There Is Much to Learn

You: "**If you just became a child of God**, that makes you a baby Christian. As such, you need to grow! Notice what helps a Christian to grow—the milk of the Word. What milk is to a baby, the Word of God is to a Christian. Will a baby be weak or strong if it does not get proper nutrition?"

Friend: "Weak."

You: "God wants you strong enough to fight off the attacks of the devil. If you read the Word of God daily and go to church regularly, you will get stronger! We've talked for quite a while already. There is a lot more to learn. I'd be willing to meet with you later this week and explain a few more things to you. What day would work best for you?"

Friend: "That would be great. I'm off on Saturday. How about then?"

You: "Sounds good! Would late morning work for you—say 11:00 o'clock?"

Friend: "That's a good time for me. Thank you so much for coming by today."

You: "No problem! Let's have a word of prayer before I leave."

Simple Soulwinning Steps

Now that you have arranged an appointment to meet again, you have set the stage to begin discipling your new convert. Let's consider that next.

Disciple

Before Jesus returned to Heaven, He charged His disciples with what has become known as the Great Commission. He said, *"Go ye therefore, and teach all nations, baptizing them in the name of the Father, and of the Son, and of the Holy Ghost: Teaching them to observe all things whatsoever I have commanded you: and, lo, I am with you alway, even unto the end of the world. Amen"* (Matthew 28:19-20). The word *teach* in verse 19 means "to disciple." Clearly, the thrust of the Great Commission is to make disciples. A disciple is a learner or follower. Following Christ begins with salvation. As we have discussed in great detail, sinners must repent of their sin and trust Jesus in order to be saved. However, making disciples does not end with showing people how to be saved. The Great Commission also charges churches to baptize believers and teach them Christ's commands.

The Purpose of Discipleship

Our duty as soulwinners does not end when people receive Christ. In fact, it has just begun. We are to encourage them to identify with Christ by obeying His

There Is Much to Learn

command to be baptized. Then we are instructed to teach them *"all things"* (Matthew 28:20). That's a big job! We cannot possibly teach *"all things"* in one or two visits. After people get saved they need consistent, systematic teaching from the Bible to enable them to grow in their faith.

A Plan for Discipleship

Try to schedule a time each week to conduct discipleship lessons with new converts. This begins by lining up an initial visit, which is usually at their home. During your first follow-up visit, answer any questions they may have. Most people will have thought a lot about what they heard the day they were saved. Then, review the plan of salvation to ensure that they really understood. It may already be apparent to you that they are truly saved by the questions they ask or comments they make at the beginning of your visit.

Bring discipleship materials with you. A good discipleship book provides prepared lessons on topics that new converts need most. When choosing discipleship books, I recommend using a short one initially. If you show up with a book that has 52 lessons, you will probably scare the people you are trying to disciple. They may quickly realize that one lesson per week for 52 weeks means that you are planning to be in their home every week for the next year. That can be

Simple Soulwinning Steps

quite intimidating! I suggest using a book that I wrote entitled *What's Next?—Important Steps for Every Believer*.[11] It reviews the plan of salvation and then provides seven key lessons that every Christian needs to know right away. One of the initial lessons is baptism. Do your best to get converts to take this important step of obedience because it will enable them to take even more steps. *What's Next?* is designed to be used with a study guide, which makes it convenient to assign questions to answer for each chapter. In seven weeks, you can complete the entire book and equip converts with essential truths to help them establish their walk with the Lord.

At the conclusion of your first follow-up visit, tell new believers that you would like to help them learn more. Offer to meet with them weekly in order to complete the book. Try to establish a definite time for your next visit. Scheduling an appointment at the same time on the same day of the week (e.g. each Tuesday at 7:00 p.m.) can help you to meet consistently.

Once converts finish *What's Next?*, they will need further instruction. A good book to consider is *The ABC's of Christian Growth* by Robert J. Sargent. It contains twenty-six lessons, which provide enough material for an additional six months. After that, you can share lessons from good Christian books, teach Bible

---

[11] *What's Next?—Important Lessons for Every Believer* by Dave Olson is available at www.help4upublications.com.

There Is Much to Learn

doctrines, or prepare practical lessons that are tailored to their specific needs.

If you do not have access to discipleship material, here are some basic topics along with verse references that can help you get started as you disciple new converts:

1. **Assurance of Salvation** – John 1:12, John 10:27-29, Ephesians 4:30, 1 Peter 1:3-5, 1 John 5:12-13

2. **Baptism** – Acts 2:38-41, Acts 8:35-39, Romans 6:3-4, John 14:15, Matthew 3:13-17

3. **Go to Church** – Hebrews 10:25, Acts 2:42, Matthew 18:20, Romans 12:4-5

4. **Read the Bible and Pray Every Day** – Psalm 119:9-11, Joshua 1:8, Jeremiah 33:3, Matthew 7:7-8, John 15:3

5. **Resist the Devil and Flee Temptation** – James 4:6-8, Ephesians 6:10-18, Mark 14:38, 1 Corinthians 10:13, 2 Corinthians 6:16-18, Romans 6:13, 16

6. **Grow as a Christian** – 2 Peter 3:18, 1 Peter 2:1-3, 2 Peter 1:5-8, Ephesians 4:15, Jude 20-21

7. **Witness to Others** – Mark 16:15, Matthew 28:19-20, Acts 1:8, Mark 1:17, Colossians 4:5-6, John 15:16

Simple Soulwinning Steps

Be flexible. Each time you meet with new converts, it can be helpful to address pressing needs that they might have in their life before presenting your planned lesson. The best way to do this is to ask them how their week went spiritually. This gives people an opportunity to share what is on their hearts. Sometimes they are in the middle of a crisis, and you may have to set aside the lesson that you planned for that week. For example, if a man's wife is threatening to leave him because he has changed so much after getting saved, he needs to know how to save his marriage more than learn about church membership! When emergencies arise, deal with them and conclude your visit by saying something like, "What we talked about this evening was really important. I'm glad you brought it up. The lesson that we were going to cover can wait until next week." This shows that you are more concerned about them than you are about your lesson. Besides, you have still discipled them by helping them to apply God's Word to their lives. Always remember that discipleship is much more than a lesson from a book. It involves learning practical truths from the best Book—the Bible!

The Patience of Discipleship

Never be discouraged with slow progress in new converts. It may seem that they only take baby steps, but at least they are steps forward! At times, new

There Is Much to Learn

believers will stumble, and you must be available to lovingly help them back up. Don't forget how long it took you to grow as a Christian. Since you have learned many valuable lessons in your walk with the Lord, you can pass them along to others. The task of making disciples out of new converts may not be easy, but it surely is rewarding! Remember Paul's exhortation— *"And let us not be weary in well doing: for in due season we shall reap, if we faint not"* (Galatians 6:9).

Final Thoughts

Throughout the pages of this book, we have covered many valuable truths about evangelizing the lost. The need of the unbelievers has been presented. Detailed instructions have been given. You know what to do and what to say in order to begin winning souls. There's only one thing left now—do something with what you have learned! *"But be ye doers of the word, and not hearers only, deceiving your own selves"* (James 1:22). God has promised to strengthen you, guide you, and accompany you. Jesus said, *"Go ye therefore...lo, I am with you alway"* (Matthew 28:19-20). Believe it and act upon it.

Take some soulwinning steps today!

APPENDIX A

Witnessing Helps

Step #1: Explain that all people have sinned.

Verses Showing the Fact of Sin	Verses for Those Who Do Not Admit Being a Sinner
1. Romans 3:10	1. 1 John 1:8, 10
2. Romans 3:23	2. Revelation 21:8
3. Isaiah 53:6	3. Romans 1:29-32
4. Isaiah 64:6	4. Galatians 5:19-21

Step #2: Explain that God punishes people with sin.

Verses for Showing the Judgment of Sin	
1. Romans 6:23	5. Luke 16:19-26
2. Romans 5:12	6. Isaiah 66:24
3. Revelation 20:12, 14	7. Psalm 9:17
4. Matthew 25:41	8. Luke 13:3

Step #3: Determine what a person is trusting to be saved and prove to him that his works cannot save him.

Verses for Showing What Cannot Save People		
Ten Commandments	Good Works	Baptism*
1. Acts 13:38-39	1. Ephesians 2:8-9	1. John 3:3-6
2. Romans 3:20, 28	2. Titus 3:5	2. Acts 2:41
3. Romans 10:3-4	3. Romans 3:12	3. Acts 8:36-37
4. Galatians 2:16, 21	4. Romans 4:1-7	4. 1 John 1:7
5. Galatians 3:10-11	5. Romans 11:6	5. Luke 7:37-50
6. Galatians 3:24-26	6. Isaiah 64:6	6. Luke 18:13-14
7. Galatians 5:4	7. Matthew 7:22-23	7. Luke 18:35-43
8. Philippians 3:9	8. 2 Timothy 1:9	8. Luke 23:39-43

* Some references for baptism show people who got saved without baptism!

Cut Along This Line and Keep Page In Your Bible for Quick Reference

Step #4: **Explain that our works do not save but Jesus does as our Substitute.**

Verses for Showing Substitution	
1. Romans 5:6, 8	3. 2 Corinthians 5:21
2. Isaiah 53:6	4. 1 Peter 3:18

Verses for Showing that Only Jesus Saves	
1. John 1:12	5. John 11:25-26
2. John 3:16, 36	6. John 14:6
3. John 5:24	7. John 20:31
4. John 10:9	8. Romans 10:9-10

Step #5: **Explain repentance.**

- Repentance is a change of mind. People must change their mind about their sin and God, desiring forgiveness.
- Mark 1:15 – Jesus taught that a person must repent and believe the gospel.

Step #6: **Ask the person if they are ready to repent and trust Jesus for salvation.**

- If so, the person can open the door and ask Jesus to save him. (Revelation 3:20, Romans 10:13)

Step #7: **Explain how to receive Jesus as Savior.**

- Share an example prayer at this time, explaining it as you go along. Ask the person if the prayer expresses the desire of his heart. If so, encourage him to receive Jesus.
- If the person needs help with a prayer, stress that your prayer cannot save them. You may assist him by having him repeat a prayer after you, going phrase by phrase.

> *Dear Jesus, I know that I have sinned against You and deserve to be punished. I am sorry for my sin and realize that I cannot save myself by doing good works. Please come into my life, save me, and change me. Right now, I receive You as my Savior. Thank You for saving me. Amen.*

APPENDIX B

Ideas for Witnessing to Non-Religious People

In Lesson 5, we discussed how to witness to people who lack a foundation of Biblical truth. The following is a gospel tract that I wrote which may provide some helpful ideas when witnessing to such individuals.

What's the Bible All About?

The Bible is the most read book in history. What makes it so special is that it's God's message to mankind. It provides the answers to questions asked by people of all walks of life such as, "Why am I here?" and "Is there life after death?" The Bible gives us not only a moral compass for life but also a solution for when we sin. Thus, it provides peace and forgiveness. The practical wisdom found in the Bible equips us to be honest, work hard, manage our finances, be kind to others, and have happy homes. The Bible has brought hope and comfort to millions of people and can do the same for you.

An Overview of the Bible

Let's allow the Bible to speak for itself—*"All scripture is given by inspiration of God, and is profitable for doctrine, for reproof, for correction, for instruction in righteousness"* (2 Timothy 3:16). The Bible consists of sixty-six books with two major divisions: the Old Testament and the New Testament. The Old Testament records the account of creation, God's laws, man's disobedience, and judgment. It includes the history of the Jewish people and prophecies of a coming Messiah. The New Testament reveals Jesus as the promised Messiah and provides encouragement and guidance for all who repent of their sin and accept Him as their Savior. The New Testament also includes prophecies involving the end of the world and what follows thereafter.

The Bible Tells Us Who God Is

God is the Creator of the universe. The very first line of the Bible declares, *"In the beginning God created the heaven and the earth"* (Genesis 1:1). It makes sense that God would explain how we got here, and He did so right away. Surely, He knew that people would develop theories such as the Big Bang that, if believed, would cast doubt on the accuracy of the rest of the Bible. However, even common sense teaches that an explosion creates disorder, not order. God has given everyone a

Appendix B

conscience that tells them that there is a Creator. *"For the invisible things of him from the creation of the world are clearly seen, being understood by the things that are made, even his eternal power and Godhead; so that they are without excuse"* (Romans 1:20). Since we all have been given the knowledge that God created us, we have no excuse to ignore Him. Because He is the Creator, He knows what is best for us and has made rules for us to follow.

The Bible Tells Us What God Is Like

It is sad that people are quick to blame God for all of the problems in the world. He did not make evil. He created a perfect world—*"And God saw every thing that he had made, and, behold, it was very good"* (Genesis 1:31). There was no sin, sickness, or sadness. Everything was *"very good."* What ruined things? Satan tempted mankind to sin, and we have all disobeyed since. The evil in this world has resulted from sin, not from God. The Lord is incapable of doing anything wrong—*"He is the Rock, his work is perfect: for all his ways are judgment: a God of truth and without iniquity, just and right is he"* (Deuteronomy 32:4). He is without sin. He is fair. He is always right. Further, *"God is love"* (1 John 4:8). He is not the source of darkness—*"God is light, and in him is no darkness at all"* (1 John 1:5). God wants the best for us, but disobedience to His laws has brought great trouble to our society. Just think how wonderful the world would be if everybody kept the Ten Commandments—there would be no murder, no stealing, and no lying. Children would obey their parents, spouses would be faithful to one another, and people would stay out of debt because they would not be covetous! Surely, God's laws are wise.

The Bible Tells Us What Man Is Like

As we have already seen, we are disobedient. While we may have a high opinion of ourselves, we also know our failures. God does too. He said, *"For all have sinned, and come short of the glory of God"* (Romans 3:23). It is not just "the other guy" who is guilty of sin. It is all of us. No matter how hard we try, we still mess up. The truth is that we cannot fix things. We have broken God's laws and need His forgiveness.

The Bible Tells Us About Judgment

Failure to find God's forgiveness leads to judgment. There is a penalty to pay for sin. *"For the wages of sin is death"* (Romans 6:23). This death refers to eternal destruction—*"And death and hell were cast into the lake of fire. This is the second death"* (Revelation 20:14). Because God loves us, He does not want us to suffer. So, He gave us the Bible to warn us of the consequences of our sin and to tell of His way of forgiveness.

Appendix B

The Bible Tells Us What God Did For Us

As you may know, the Bible declares the Trinity of God. Like we have three parts to us (body, soul, and spirit), He also is three in one (the Father, the Son, and the Holy Spirit). Consider how much God loved us. *"For God so loved the world, that he gave his only begotten Son, that whosoever believeth in him should not perish, but have everlasting life"* (John 3:16). Jesus (the Son) left Heaven, came to earth, lived a perfect life, and took our punishment upon Himself when He died on the cross. Because God is just, He has to punish sin. However, because He is love, He became our Substitute. *"For he* [the Father] *hath made him* [Jesus] *to be sin for us, who knew no sin; that we might be made the righteousness of God in him"* (2 Corinthians 5:21). Though we are sinners, we can become righteous by asking Jesus to be our Savior!

The Bible Tells Us How to Be Saved

Because Jesus paid for our sins, it reminds us that we cannot pay for them ourselves. No amount of good works we do can earn forgiveness. Instead, Jesus mentioned two requirements to be saved—*"...repent ye, and believe the gospel"* (Mark 1:15). First, we must *"repent,"* meaning that we change our mind. When we realize that our sin offends God, we should hate it and desire to be cleansed. Second, we must *"believe the*

Simple Soulwinning Steps

gospel." The gospel refers to Christ's death, burial, and resurrection. If you believe that Jesus died for you and rose again, you can have eternal life.

Are you ready to accept God's gift of salvation by receiving Jesus as your personal Savior? If so, He is ready to forgive and change you. We are promised, *"For whosoever shall call upon the name of the Lord shall be saved"* (Romans 10:13).

You can call upon Him to save you by praying something like this: *Dear Jesus, I realize I have broken your commandments and face eternal punishment. I am sorry for sinning against you and believe that you died in my place. Please forgive my sin and save my soul. I trust you alone for salvation. Thank you, Jesus. Amen.*

ABOUT THE AUTHOR

Dave Olson became a Baptist preacher in 1993 and has served the Lord in many capacities since that time. After teaching in Bible college, heading up a Christian school, and serving as a pastor, God called Dave into missions. He and his family faithfully served the Lord as missionaries to Zambia, Africa for ten years until a series of ongoing health problems and life-threatening illnesses led to their return in 2012.

In early 2013, the Lord led Dave to focus on a writing ministry, and his books are now used at home and abroad. Dave's experience as an educator and preacher has uniquely equipped him to communicate God's truths to people from every walk of life. In addition to his writing ministry, Dave preaches in revivals, missions conferences, and special meetings across the country.

Visit www.help4Upublications.com for more titles.

Other Titles Available on www.help4Upublications.com

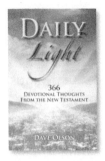

Reading the Word of God is the best way to start your day, and *Daily Light* can make it easier! This book can be used for either personal or family devotions to provide practical insight for daily living. It embarks on a journey through the New Testament, including one thought from an assigned daily Scripture reading designed to share either a challenge or a promise for the day. (204 pages)

Get ready to take a journey through many of the Old Testament books. Morning Light starts in Genesis and includes the books of the Law, History, and Prophets. A practical thought from an assigned daily Scripture reading will challenge you each day. Whether you choose to use Morning Light for personal or family devotions, you will develop a better understanding of the Bible and find practical insight for daily living. (206 pages)

Have you ever wondered what God has to say about finances? It's time to learn the proven principles of Scripture concerning money management. Money by the Book provides Biblical solutions for you and your money. Chapters on contentment, giving, saving, getting out of debt, setting up a budget, teaching your children about money, how to reduce spending, and much more! *Money by the Book* is now being used as a textbook in Bible colleges. (246 pages)

Nobody is exempt from heartaches and hardships. Even great heroes of the faith battled their emotions. Throughout the history of the world, people have battled grief, discouragement, fear, and anxiety. When handled correctly, trials can draw us closer to the Lord and build our faith. Learn how to see your trials as God sees them and react as He has instructed. When you do, you will see brighter days ahead! (188 pages)

Made in the USA
Middletown, DE
02 April 2025